Humans and Change
Seven Ideas out of the Ordinary

Humans and Change
Seven Ideas out of the Ordinary

Charles Oxnard
University of Western Australia, Australia

"There are so many patterns and connections between art, science and nature. They forever evolve, adapt and change. This is vital for all of us".

Josie Mitchell (UK Artist)

World Scientific

Published by

World Scientific Publishing Co. Pte. Ltd.
5 Toh Tuck Link, Singapore 596224
USA office: 27 Warren Street, Suite 401-402, Hackensack, NJ 07601
UK office: 57 Shelton Street, Covent Garden, London WC2H 9HE

British Library Cataloguing-in-Publication Data
A catalogue record for this book is available from the British Library.

HUMANS AND CHANGE
SEVEN IDEAS OUT OF THE ORDINARY

Copyright © 2024 by World Scientific Publishing Co. Pte. Ltd.

All rights reserved. This book, or parts thereof, may not be reproduced in any form or by any means, electronic or mechanical, including photocopying, recording or any information storage and retrieval system now known or to be invented, without written permission from the publisher.

For photocopying of material in this volume, please pay a copying fee through the Copyright Clearance Center, Inc., 222 Rosewood Drive, Danvers, MA 01923, USA. In this case permission to photocopy is not required from the publisher.

ISBN 978-981-12-8308-6 (hardcover)
ISBN 978-981-12-8390-1 (paperback)
ISBN 978-981-12-8309-3 (ebook for institutions)
ISBN 978-981-12-8310-9 (ebook for individuals)

For any available supplementary material, please visit
https://www.worldscientific.com/worldscibooks/10.1142/13587#t=suppl

Preface

Ideas about human change cover the spectrum from the fictions of Pellucidar (Edgar Rice Burroughs) and Avatar (James Cameron), through the *Shape of Things to Come* (H. G. Wells), to the *End of History and the Last Man* (Francis Fukuyama).

Many people today deny the idea of human evolution. Many others, accepting that humans have changed in the past, do not see change as still occurring. My challenge is, not only that we humans are still changing, but that we are changing ever more rapidly, and in new ways.

Is *Homo sapiens* (vainly named, wise human) already in the process of becoming *Homo sapientior* (wiser human)? Can we expect further change to *Homo sapientissimus* (wisest human)?

And do we have to fear regression to *Homo nerdensis*?

Some such changes may come (unwittingly) from our own hands. They challenge the constraints of the conventional wisdoms, gold standards, and straightjackets of the usual human evolution story. I especially worry about such constraints in the teaching of STEM (Science, Technology, Engineering and Mathematics). This is especially so if we recognize that, as seen through the eyes of an old professor, STEM really means $S(S)TE(AH)M(M)$. The bracketed parts, $(S)(AH)(M)$, of this new (but awkward) acronym, stand for the generally forgotten, but especially creative components of learning: Social Sciences, Arts, Humanities and Medicine.

This book thus starts with some unconventional ideas on the human condition that have arisen from my personal teaching, research and service, from the work of many students, colleagues and mentors, from collaborations with workers in disciplines completely different than my own (statistics, mathematics, physics, engineering, computer analyses and modelling), and from people outside academia (in industry, business and government).

It considers some 'out of the ordinary' ideas about sex and gender, race and ethnicity, kindreds and ancestors, aging and death, and brain and mind. Are such ideas merely figments of my imagination? Or could they really have unsuspected but major implications for a changing world?

Economist Ray Dalio has recently spoken to the past, present and future of nations. As an economist, he defines the major factors that have raised some nations up and pushed some down. Of course, we would expect that an economist's first factors would be economics and disorder. Surprisingly, however, he also recognizes an unusual third, education: the effects on nations of changes in finding new knowledge and challenging the old!

As a result, this book ends with ideas about the implications of damaging changes to the human condition, especially recently, and especially in the West. Can anything be done to repair these problems? And to take us to a new, higher level?

These thoughts have further matured through a decade of popular talks on science and medicine that I have given to MALA (Mature Adult Learning Association) in Western Australia. MALA people are all old, most retired, some long since retired, many originally professionals, a majority of women (of course), but all still keenly interested in what is going on in the world, all participating so wonderfully in discussions, all wanting to keep their brains alive. (Do they realize, I wonder, that they help keep my brain alive?)

Contents

Preface		v
Chapter 1	How Do You Get Ideas, Daddy?	1
Chapter 2	Ideas about Sex: Yesterday, Today and Tomorrow	27
Chapter 3	More on Sex: Yesterday's Changes	39
Chapter 4	Ideas about Gender: Women's Struggles (and Men's)!	51
Chapter 5	Dangerous Differences: Race and Ethnicity, Kindred and Ancestors	75
Chapter 6	Aging and Death: Life Span, Mortality, Wellness and Illness!	117
Chapter 7	Human Brains: Not Just Bigger — Changed, Changing, Unique!	143
Chapter 8	Progress of Ideas: Challenge, Threat and Glory?	183
Chapter 9	Failure of Ideas: Cheating, Damned Cheating and 'Chorruption'	189
Chapter 10	My Mistakes: Ideas I Missed!	207
Chapter 11	An Eighth Idea out of the Ordinary: Damages to Learning!	229

Chapter 1
How Do You Get Ideas, Daddy?

An innocent question from my two small sons as I walked with them to the Laboratory School at The University of Chicago during the record snows of our first weeks there in November, 1966. I know this, because, unbeknownst to me at the time, one of their teachers was walking behind us, listening!

One often thinks first of the well-known people who have been responsible for one's ideas. Yet my first ideas came from the enthusiasm of a relatively unknown headmaster of a tiny primary school in the 1940s in Gullane, East Lothian, Scotland.

In that school, the education was very classical. The subjects taught were: English (mainly English grammar taught the Scottish way: how useful that turned out to be for an academic career); geography (mainly Scottish geography): how many times did I draw the outline of Scotland, I could almost do it in my sleep; history, mainly Scottish history: when we did Bannockburn (where the Scots defeated the English) I was okay, but the day we did Flodden Field (where the English beat the Scots), as the only English boy in a Scottish school, that was the day that I had to run home (luckily, I was long and thin and fast); and mathematics: (one could be stopped by the headmaster to do 'ten mental' anywhere in the school, even in the playground, and at any time of the day).

"But," the headmaster also said to me, "there are other subjects that we do not teach. One is a thing called science".

He may have seen how interested I was in his curio cabinet (displaying a kukri and kris, a blown ostrich egg, some animal skulls, and a theodolite [whatever that was to this small boy], all picked up during an earlier military career abroad). It was true: I spent hours looking in that cabinet and dreaming.

In other words, that headmaster understood, somehow, what interested that small boy. "You'd better be reading these", he said, throwing at me works (in English, of course) by Goethe, Wegener, D'Arcy Thompson, and Solly Zuckerman.

Thus, in 1942, at age nine, knowing nothing of literary Goethe's Faust, I totally 'bought' anatomist Goethe's idea that the skull was simply a series of fused segments (Figure 1.1).

As a result, Goethe wrote to a colleague:

"I have found neither gold nor silver,
but something that unspeakably delights me, Eureka!
Only, I beg of you, not a word, for this must be a great secret!
It is the keystone to human evolution."

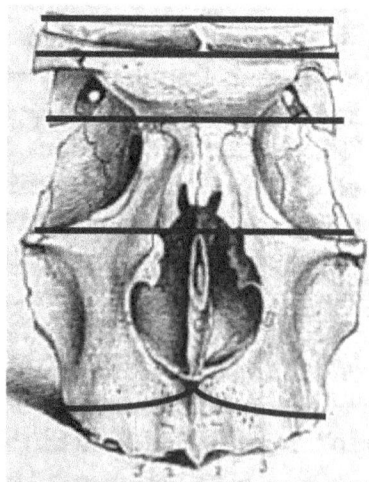

Fig. 1.1. Goethe's idea of segments in the skull.

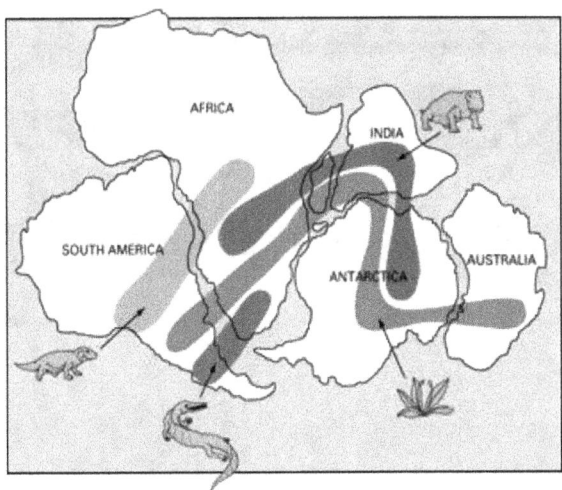

Fig. 1.2. Wegener's early twentieth century idea of the movements of the continents before plate tectonics.

This excited me. I did not know, of course, that others (e.g. Oken) had also had this idea much earlier. Nor did I know that it was wrong, until I later came to read Gavin de Beer's tome on the vertebrate skull at university in 1954. Goethe and Oken were both wrong. But today's developmental biology shows that they were both a little bit more right than most of us thought at the time.

In 1942, also, I may have been the only person in the world who did not know that Wegener's idea of the movements of the continents (Figure 1.2) was **not accepted**. It was only in 1952, by the time I got to university, that everyone else had become excited by **plate tectonics**. I was so surprised. I had always known it was so!

In 1942, further, though I could not possibly understand the mathematical formulae, and Greek and Latin quotations in D'Arcy Thompson's wonderful book *On Growth and Form,* I adored it. There was so much in that book to touch a nine-year-old.

Fig. 1.3. Interior of a vulture's wing bone from D'Arcy Thompson.

Fig. 1.4. A forerunner to the Spitfire with struts 'between' the wings just like (as a small boy saw it) the struts 'within' the wings of the bird. Of course, I had it wrong!

For example, the struts in the interior of a bird's wing (Figure 1.3) were so like the struts in the wings of the biplanes of my childhood days (Figure 1.4). And I even had a photograph of a Walrus (a biplane with a backwards pointing engine) that had landed upside down in the Solent, the sea inlet at Southampton where we lived before the war. But my copy of that picture has long since vanished. Figure 1.5, showing it lifted out of the water, is all Google can show me!

Fig. 1.5. It doesn't always work: a Walrus, forerunner of the Spitfire, being hauled up out of the Solent. It had landed in the inlet upside down!

This was all so exciting, to a boy whose father had worked on the Spitfire, first at Supermarine Works, Southampton, before WW2, and later, during the war, as Vickers Armstrong's Representative for Scotland on the Ministry of Aircraft Production.

And again, D'Arcy Thompson's pictures showing the similarity between animal backbones and cantilever bridges were fascinating. Of course, I was especially aware of the cantilever bridge over the river Forth, just down the Firth, from our wartime home in East Lothian, Scotland (Figure 1.6).

I knew then so little about these things that I was not aware that this was a spurious comparison. It looked good to me.

It was, however, Thompson's pictures of the use of Cartesian coordinate transformation diagrams, borrowed from the art of Albrecht Dürer (Figure 1.7) to help draw faces, and his own application to helping in understand the shapes of fishes

6   *Humans and Change: Seven Ideas out of the Ordinary*

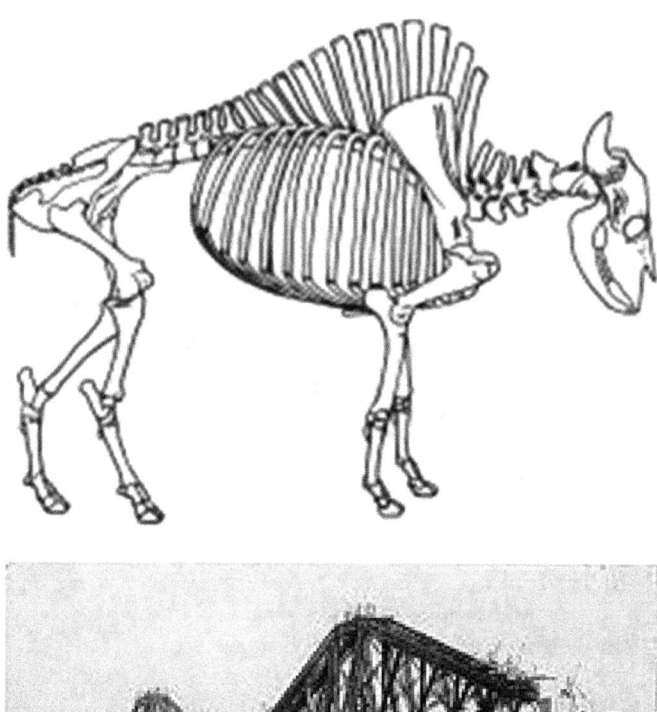

Fig. 1.6. Darcy Thompson's comparison of the (above) vertebral column of a bison and (below) the cantilever structure of the Forth Bridge under construction.

(Figure 1.7), that excited me most. Using this idea from art, Thompson 'described' (showed) how one fish can be 'transformed' into another. Of course, both Dürer and Thompson used pencil and paper to present these differences.

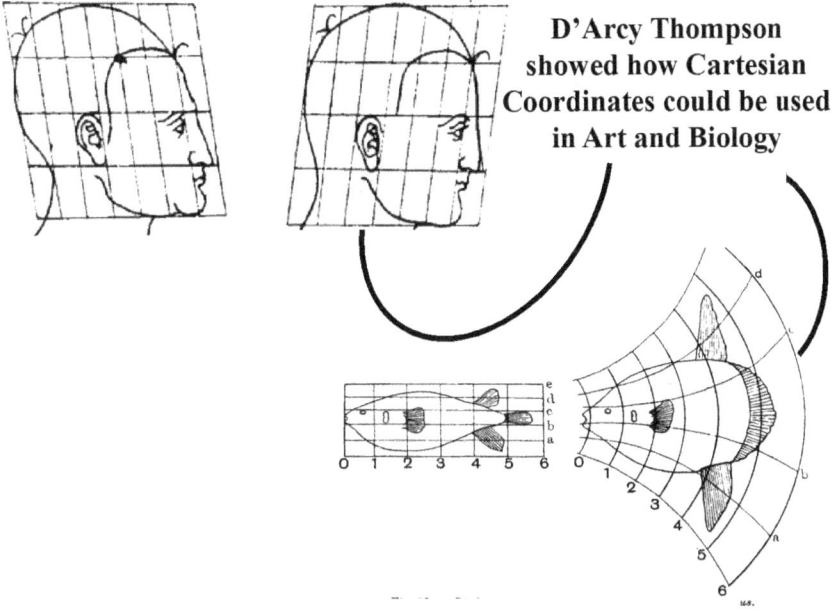

Fig. 1.7. Comparisons of faces using a Cartesian transformation (Albrecht Dürer as cited by D'Arcy Thompson). Cartesian transformations of fishes by D'Arcy Thompson, 1917.

Years later (in the 1960s), also **with pencil and paper**, I borrowed the idea to compare differences in shoulder blades in monkeys and apes (upper frame, Figure 1.8). My contribution was double. I borrowed the idea of **the transformation to compare bone shapes.** But I also thought that they **suggested bone functions.** But how good was this — I was not certain until 40 years later when, with Gene Albrecht (originally one of my research students in Chicago in the 60s), the same thing was done **computationally through thin plate splines**, and, happily, with a similar result (lower frame, Figure 1.8).

So in 1955 I borrowed his idea to compare shoulder blades

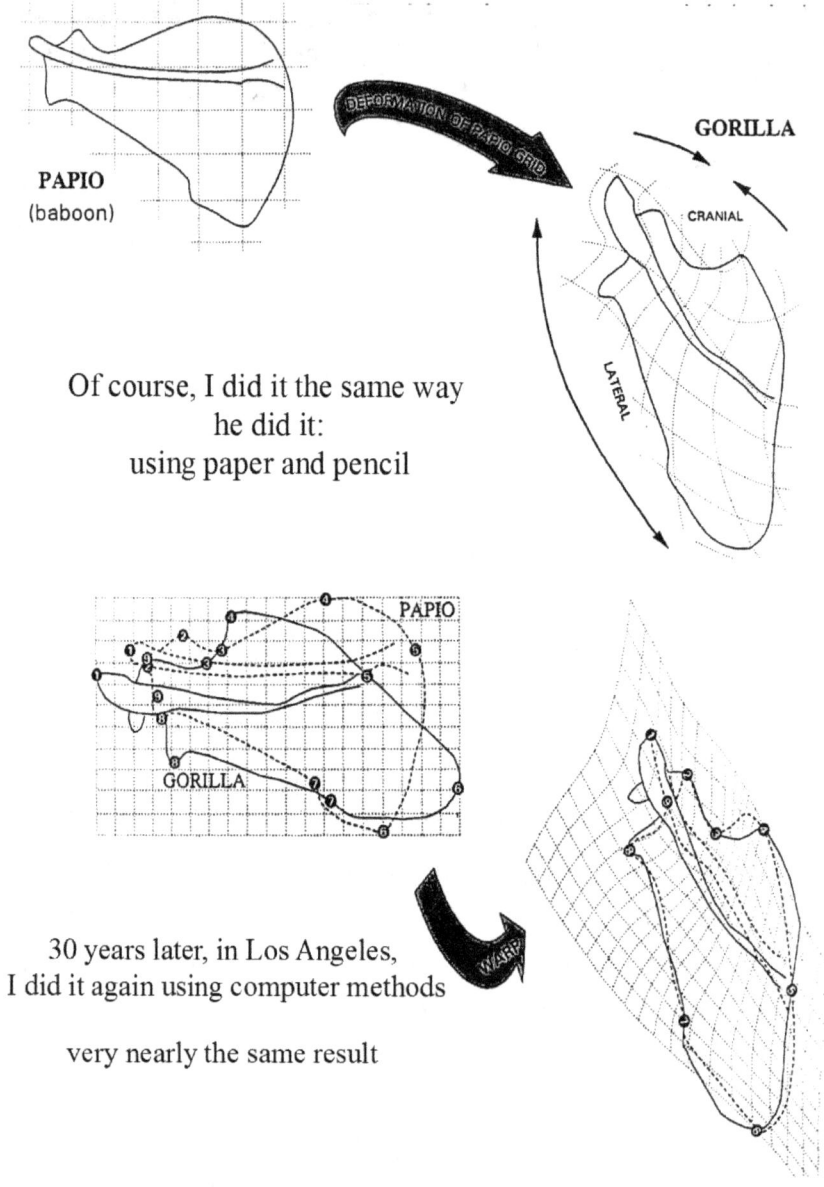

Of course, I did it the same way
he did it:
using paper and pencil

30 years later, in Los Angeles,
I did it again using computer methods

very nearly the same result

Fig. 1.8. Cartesian transformations (upper frame) and thin plate splines (lower frame).

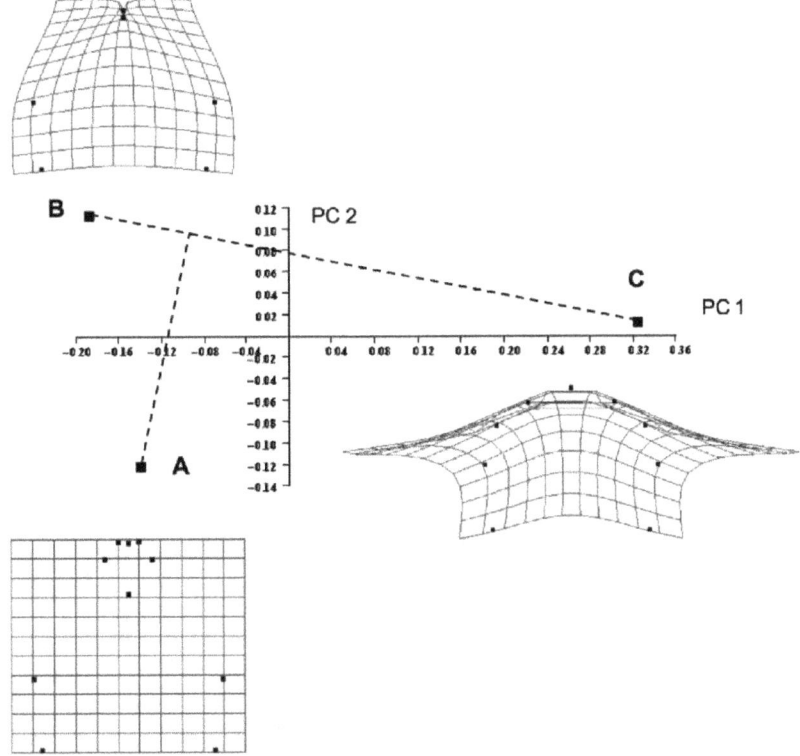

Fig. 1.9. The **simplicity of differences in skull shape** between a human (A) a chimpanzee (B) and a gorilla, (C) when based upon geometric landmarks defining simple lengths and widths (simple shape).

These ideas of the value of the combination of science and art, especially so now **when the broad idea of the liberal arts seems to be disappearing from education**, have been with me ever since reading that book as a schoolboy.

Many years later, Paul O'Higgins (at the University of York) and I used later developments of these ideas to compare skulls of humans and apes (Figures 1.9 and 1.10). Incredible complexities of form were revealed.

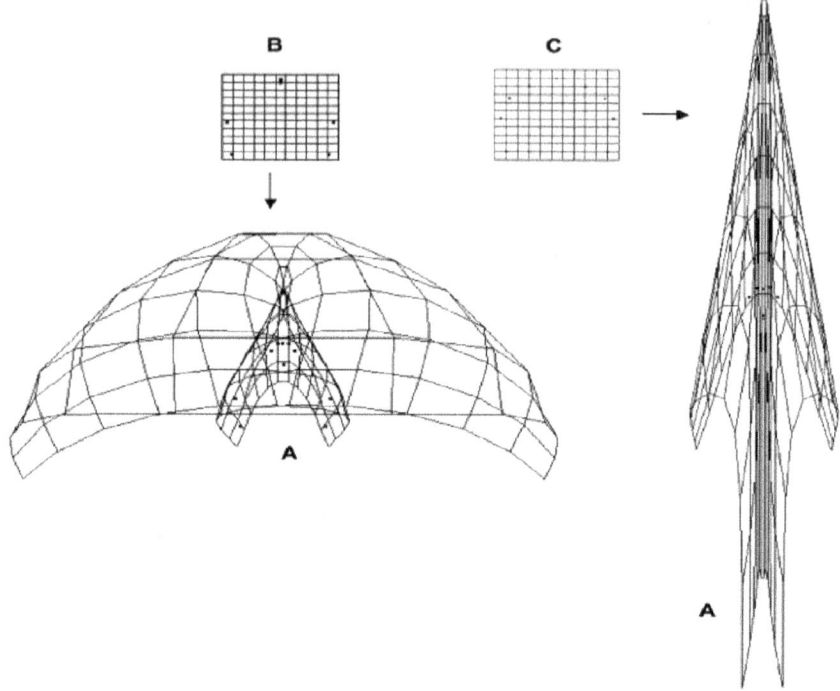

Fig. 1.10. The complexities of these same skull shapes when based upon landmarks related to bone, joint and muscle attachments **reflecting function.**

Over the years, I have followed up these ideas borrowing many other methods: optical Fourier functions, computational fast Fourier transforms, Buckminster Fuller's 'tensegrity' concepts, engineering Finite Element analyses, and Thom's catastrophe theory, among others (see Figure 1.11).

Once again, artistic ideas were helping to inform scientific concepts. The methods of art can be so valuable in science; or, to put it another way, they show how science can mirror art! Such ideas allow us to visualize the changes in one thing over several times, the differences between several things at the same time, or both together.

Do mathematical figures like these have any potential, possibly just descriptive, possibly biologically explanatory, in dealing with novelty, loss, and discontinuities in anatomical structure, in biological function, in development and growth, and in evolution? Our work suggests that such methods may be useful, or should, at the very least, be tried!

Finally, there was that 1934 book by Dr. Zuckerman (as he was then, Figure 1.12): *The Functional Affinities of Man, Monkeys and Apes*. It completely fascinated me. However, though there

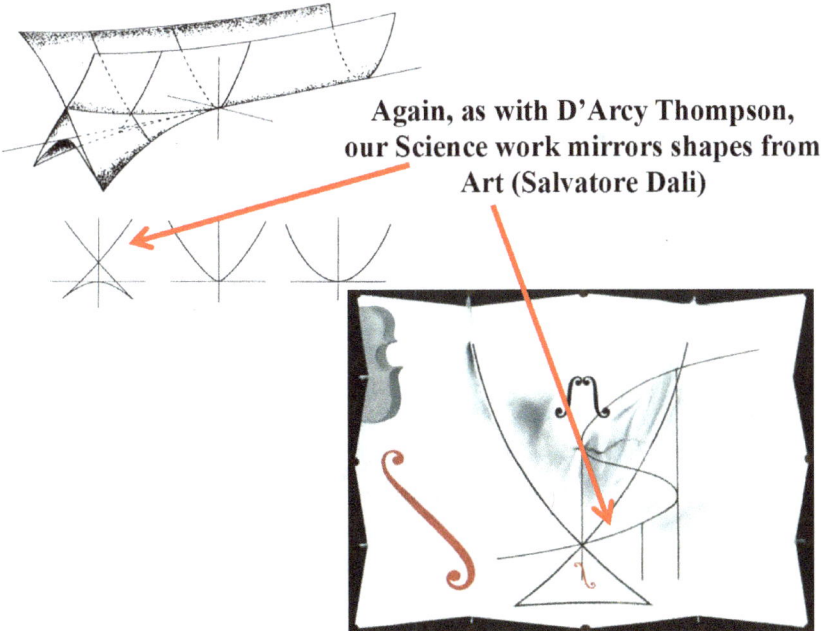

Fig. 1.11. Upper figures: two catastrophe diagrams in science (from Thom), and a 'catastrophe figure' in art (by Salvador Dalí). Middle figures: visualizing changes during development and evolution shown as the crest on a diagram of a 'real' wave breaking, together with the changes at particular points along the wave crest. Lower figures: further transformations (swallowtail hyperbolics, swallowtail elliptics and butterfly parabolics), also redrawn from Thom's work, representing the development of a series of possible foldings (umbilici).

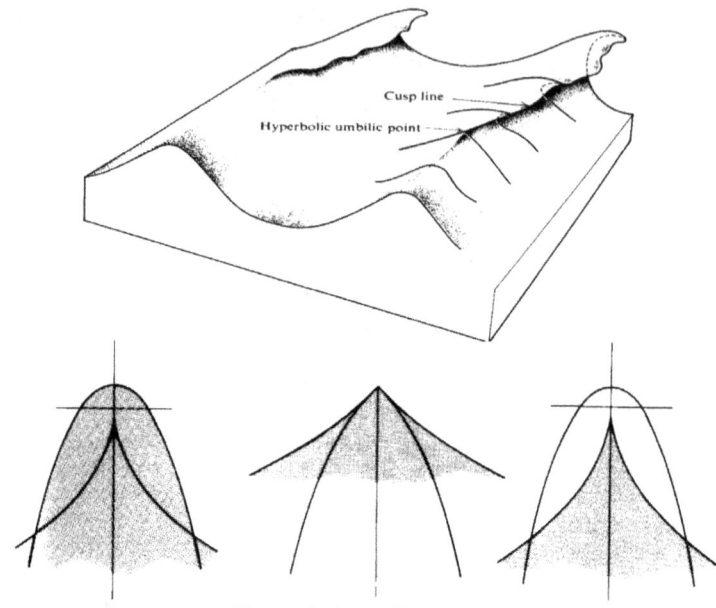

Changes in form of Wave Crest

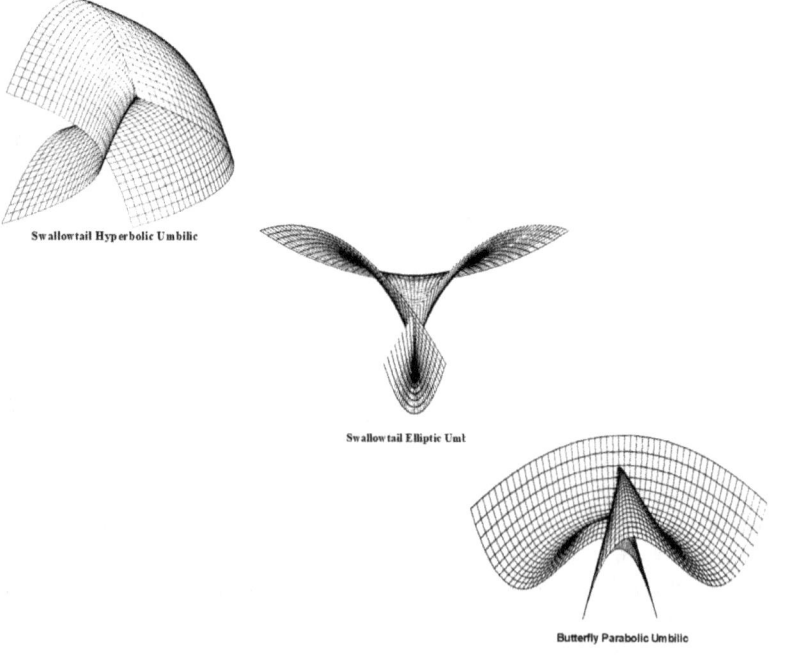

Swallowtail Hyperbolic Umbilic

Swallowtail Elliptic Umb

Butterfly Parabolic Umbilic

Fig. 1.11. (*Continued*)

Fig. 1.12. Solly Zuckerman.

were many pictures in it, in this case it was the words that took my attention.

Thus, in 1933, the then Dr. Zuckerman wrote:

"New students will accept without question evolutionary relationships in which the anatomical differences between two separate types may be less than the differences between two specimens of a single type ... they may automatically draw distorted evolutionary conclusions."

And Zuckerman went on to point out that:

*"Anatomical differences are perhaps the least indicators of evolutionary relationships
... a host of other differentiations could be more important ...
reproductive mechanisms, blood reactions, brain functions, behaviour patterns, genetics of affinity and divergence, even diseases and parasites."*

How percipient those 1933 words sound in the light of today's understanding of evolution. Of course, I then knew little of this. But, even then, these words excited me!

That Scottish headmaster never knew I would later work with that 'Dr.' Zuckerman!

How silly, for a school boy to think he could collaborate with such a distinguished individual: Solly Zuckerman, doctor of medicine, later professor of anatomy, later still Fellow of the Royal Society, peer of the realm, confidant of prime ministers, friend of monarchs!

Yet I did work with him, from my being a student in 1952 until his death in 1993 age 88.

Dr. Watson, that little old Scottish schoolmaster, can have had no idea of the lifetime effect his suggestions would have on that small boy.

But today I ask: why, on Earth, in 1942, did Dr. Watson not give me another book: Charles Robert Darwin's *On the Origin of Species*?

(Perhaps his Scottish religion got in the way?)

Many Years Pass, and We Come to California

A hundred miles down the coast from Los Angeles is the Institute for Creation Science. They were delighted at my arrival in California in 1978. After all, isn't Oxnard a scientist who debunks Darwinism? Isn't Oxnard therefore anti-evolution? Isn't his work therefore supporting evidence for creation science?!

Googling my name in earlier times would yield several hundred hits on my anatomical researches. There were also, naturally, many hits on the City of Oxnard in California. But thousands of hits were specifically about how my work (and that of Zuckerman, Ashton, Lisowski, and many other colleagues and students), because we *test (read 'attack') human evolution*, must therefore *support (read 'confirm') creation science*! And there is nothing I can do about it. You try removing rubbish from the internet!

More Years Pass and We Arrive in Australia

In the USA at that time, the winning of research funds had gradually become harder and harder (until one's eventual 'take' was reduced to only one in every four or five applications). Therefore, when I first arrived in Australia, I applied for six external research grants to make sure I could hit the research ground running. I was almost embarrassed to immediately get three! The golden age of research, dead in England, dying in the USA, was still then alive in Australia. That was AD 1987 (AD meaning Anti-Dawkins, but John not Richard!). And for thirty more years in Australia I remained lucky; external grant successes continued.

However, in contrast, my first internal research grant application at the University of Western Australia **failed**!

The next year I applied again. **Failed!**

And the year after that. **Failed!**

Then I appointed Nina Jablonski from abroad (in those days professors appointed academics). I told her this story. She smiled, gently.

"Oh," she said, "just delete the word evolution from the titles of your research proposals".

She had learned this from the Women's Group on campus, an organization to which I did not have access.

Next year proved her right! **Success!**

Also, when I came to Australia, I discovered that 43 percent of medical students in Melbourne believed in special creation (data from a questionnaire asked of Melbourne medical students by Roger Short on *his* advent in Australia). I never dared ask this question of the medical student cohorts in Western Australia!

Thus, you can see: the mores of my Scottish schoolmaster in the forties, and the US Creation Science Institute in the 70s, were still alive and well in WA in the nineties. And to some degree, it is still so today: a 'legacy' (but unwanted) of Darwin!

In Contrast: Darwin's Wanted Legacy

Darwin wrote: "All living things have much in common, in their internal metabolic processes, their ultrastructural and molecular relationships, their intra-cellular organelles and intra-nuclear complexities, their molecular genetics, their developmental and reproductive patterns, and their immunological tolerances and resistances".

But of course, **I lie**. These are all modern terms, never known by Darwin.

Darwin's actual words were:

> "All living things have much in common, in their chemical compositions, their cellular structures, their germinal vesicles, their laws of growth and reproduction, and their liabilities to injurious substances."

And his conclusion was:

> "If we admit these, we must likewise admit that all the organic beings which have ever lived on this Earth are descended from one primordial form."

Darwin's are the words, Darwin's is the book, changing forever the way we see humans. Yet Darwin and *On the Origin of Species* was very careful about human origins and change. Darwin only briefly recognized the similarities of humans and apes. He was well aware of the implications of his 'dangerous idea'. (And extraplanetary research may, even yet, prove his main thesis wrong.)

Today, David Attenborough documents this for the full sweep of life on Earth. I here summarize it for human change alone:

Ever since Darwin (famous phrase), we anatomists have been dissecting away all those bits of the human body that are common to apes and humans.

The heart, the kidneys, the liver, the lungs — they can go — essentially the same in apes and humans (even, nowadays, occasionally exchangeable through grafting!).

Muscles and bones — they can go — similar in apes and humans. (Except for a few little bits in apes: e.g. one small muscle in the arm enjoying the sonorous title of 'latissimo-dorso-condyloid-epitrochlearis' [I love long words!], and one small bone in the wrist, unknown to most doctors, the 'os centrale'). Yet the 'ghosts' of many, apparently unimportant ape structures exist, unexpectedly, in some humans!

Even the brain — that can go — 96.6 percent of the brain size in apes and humans is simply the result of the relationship between brain size and body size!

> *Is nothing left? What about behavior, relationship, taxonomy, classification?*

Thus, ever since Darwin, behaviorists have been chipping away at humans.

'Only Man' (sic) uses tools. No, lots of animals use tools.

Aha, only Man (sic) makes tools. No, many animals make tools, even some surprising ones.

Aha, aha, only Man (sic) makes tools for future use. No, some animals do even this.

Does nothing separate us and others?

Ever since Darwin, taxonomists have demoted *Homo* (Man, sic). Demoted from our zoological superfamily (named after us, the *Hominoidea*), down to our own family (the *Hominidae*), down again to our own subfamily (the *Homininae*), down, again, to our own species (*Homo sapiens*). We are even relegated by some all the way down to mere subspecies status *Homo sapiens sapiens*, alongside others, such as *Homo sapiens neanderthalensis*.

And all the way down we have been trailed by the apes.
Some have even wanted to include some apes in the genus Homo!

And after Darwin?

I have one distinguished colleague (Professor Alan Harvey) who has suggested (with help from a classical scholar, and a little tongue in cheek) elevating *Homo sapiens* (Man [sic] the Wise) of yesterday, to *Homo sapientior* (Man [sic] the Wiser) of today. Would this be a new species, I wondered?! Could the ghosts of yesteryear be pointing towards visions for the future?

Could modern humans actually split? I do not mean into the Morlocks and Eloi of H. G. Wells' *Time Machine*, but from *Homo sapientior* (above) into both *Homo sapientissimus* (Man [sic] the 'Wisest') and *Homo nerdensis* (Man [sic] the 'Nerd').

These last might be in a transition from the Fishing-Net and the Butterfly-Net, to the 'InterNet' and the 'TwitterNet'! **This would be human change continuing, and very differently, from other creatures!**

Of course, when I was a scientific child, I accepted, as a child of that day, that the common ancestor of modern humans and modern apes lived 20, 25 or even 30 million years ago. This was a respectable degree of distance. One that the 'bishop's (Wilberforce's) wife' could tolerate. She is supposed to have exclaimed:

"I hear Mr. Darwin has said that we may be descended from an Ape.
I hope that it be not true.
But if it be true, I pray that it become not widely known!"

But when I became a scientific man, I put away childish things. New ideas from fossil anatomies, animal behaviors, molecular structures, and brain sizes, seem to have been drawing the human/ape relationship ever closer — at one point to less than 3 million years! The culmination of this trend is the oft-quoted DNA factoid that humans are 98.6 percent chimpanzees. (Of course, we are also 96 percent orangutans, 90 percent rats, and even 55 percent bananas.)

Now, in my scientific dotage, I perceive a reversal. New fossils, new behaviors, and new molecules are pushing our common ancestry with the apes further back — back from the three-million-year figure, back to five million years, eight million, ten million — and most recently — perhaps even back to more than threeen million years. **Are we actually so much more different from the apes?**

Of course, not all of our parts are different from apes! Human livers, kidneys, spleens, bloods, bones, etc., are all similar to ape and monkey livers, kidneys, spleens, bloods, bones, etc. It is only when we come to brains that our findings imply that humans are markedly different. Human brains are, by our measures, an incredible 20 times more different from ape and monkey brains, than these latter are from each other.

And human brains may have been changing even more quickly, perhaps, recently, as much as 20 times more quickly, than ape and monkey brains!

Implications for Humans?

Could this view lead to the idea of a new form of evolution? One not available to animals, due to the interactions of genetic blueprints, developmental processes, and environmental factors, in a species that is capable of additional changes that we, as humans, alone, can make in ourselves?

Such changes (initially unwitting, of course) have occurred down the generations, along the families, across the communities, and among the tribes. They derive both from guarding tradition, knowledge and history of the old, and through discovery and teaching of the new. They involved, initially, the use of pictures, symbols, music and rhythms, at first in temporary form: marks in the sand, sound in the air, light in the eye, passed contemporaneously between communicating individuals. Later, they were passed on more permanently through the medium of the rock engraving and painting, the dried mud tablet, the vellum, the book, the gramophone record, and the cinematographic film.

Now, today and finally tomorrow, they are being carried among us all electronically, by the computer, the iPhone, artificial intelligence, and the cloud.

All these, span an entire world, and all these, for no other creature!

It is entirely possible that the last of these items, the new 'information technology', is doing something new to the brains of the 'information generations' of *Homo sapiens*. Who amongst us has not been embarrassed by the 'teen', even the child, who knows how to 'work the machine', and who is scathing that 'nanny and grandad can't'? Would that we could cut up a few infants' brains to find out what is happening! (Of course not!) But the new non-invasive imaging methods are starting to show us!

Of course, some such changes might be strongly negative. We already hear voices warning about the dangers of such technology to the very young. Uncontrolled access to the generations of iPhones and computers by the generations of the young are producing the brains of *'Homo bully-ensis'*, *'Homo messed-up-ensis'* and *'Homo suicidal-ensis'*! Might these processes eventually give rise to the brains of *'Homo nerdensis'*?

But other changes wrought by such technologies might be extremely positive: helping produce the brains of *'Homo sapientissimus'*!

I doubt that *nerdensis* would often breed with *sapientissimus*. Nerds seem so often to suffer from such major behavioral problems (for example, even in just getting on with their peers, never mind their parents) that such interbreeding might well be reduced, or might not even occur. (Tongue in cheek here, because, through sex, almost anything can happen!)

Yet the new improvements in women's education and careers, together with the relative reductions in female numbers in many societies, seem to be associated with the fewer women seeking out, among the many men, only those educated at their own level or above. Are 'lesser males' being socially removed from the breeding pools of these fewer but 'super women'? Might these females seek only the best or none? Might they have few enough children to fall beneath the replacement number? Might this lead to new possibilities for the evolution of the human brain? Far from slowly drawing to a close as some have thought, human evolution may be opening up in new ways not apparent to Darwin. (And what about those societies that deny education for females, seeing them as only, apparently, for scut work, giving pleasure for men, and producing babies?)

Was Aldous Huxley (1946) correct in imagining his *'Alpha intellectuals'* (given extra drug stimulation in the 'artificial womb')? He was certainly right in visualizing his drug-damaged *'Delta morons'* (today's equivalent is the progeny of the alcoholic mum). Perhaps Huxley's (Julian, 1957, not Thomas Henry, of the late 1800s) idea of a new grade to life, the *Psychozoa*, containing only humans, is half legitimate! Was H. G. Wells (both himself, 1895, and his 'alter ego', David Lake, 1981) percipient in envisioning separate Eloi and Morlocks in our human future? And will nothing exist in that future if we do not get a handle on the killing of people, and the 'killing' of the planet?

What did You do in the War, Daddy?

The above heading is a second question, this time from today's great grandchild, but also, when one is older, from many people, especially when one has retired. Children, students, younger academics, people at academic social occasions, especially mature adults after public lectures, even just new friends, all ask an equivalent question. *(Of course, I was never actually in the war.)* But for years, finding an answer about my life in general has nonplussed me simply because, over a fairly long life, I seem to have done so many different things.

It all seems to have been a bit muddled.

But my wife, Eleanor, who has proofread almost all of my writings, asked me, the other day: "Why don't you write about the curious ways in which the various things you have done are linked, about the different ideas that they have suggested?" It seemed a most interesting idea!

It has led to my subtitle: **Seven Ideas** *(or perhaps some other number)* **Out of the Ordinary!**

This book thus documents the tortuous research pathways that have developed in my mind over some seventy years. It has depended first of all upon the work, over the years, of a series of teachers, colleagues and students in all aspects of human biology. Many of them fit in all three categories. They have supported me, participated with me, and indeed, often led me, in many new and different research directions.

It has also depended on many colleagues in disciplines completely different from mine, especially statistics, mathematics, physics, engineering, and modelling.

Furthermore, it has depended on many people quite outside academia, in industry, business, law, and government.

Finally, in more recent years, it has matured from a series of general talks I have given to an organization called **MALA**. This, the **M**ature **A**dult **L**earning **A**ssociation, is dedicated to providing mental stimulus, helping older people keep their brains alive. I have been most happy to be involved in these programs since 2013, run separately, in Peel, Rockingham and Manning in Western Australia (and owing much to Hazel Dawn Butorac and Joe Butorac).

My part in MALA was to give a series of talks on science and medicine to complement talks by others on a wide variety of topics. MALA individuals are all older, most retired, some long since retired, many originally professionals, a majority women (of course), all still interested in what is going on in the world, and all wanting to keep their brains alive. Did they realize, I wonder, that I did it to keep my own brain alive? All of this has also led to **Seven (or perhaps some other number) Ideas Out of the Ordinary**.

Why **Out of the Ordinary**? I have always felt that it was critical in research to follow strongly where the data led, rather than where I might hope they would lead. I have always felt it important to try hard to break the conventional wisdom, rather than trying to confirm it. I have always looked for new directions in which thinking might go, rather than following along an already plotted line or a standard graph. Such ways of thinking about, and even doing, science and medicine, mean that my ideas were (and still largely are) often contrary to the standard view, therefore out of the ordinary, even on occasion heretical, and so, sometimes, even damned!

This has been so since the beginnings of my research career. Thus, my earliest researches questioned the standard idea of the australopithecine fossils as direct human ancestors. As a result, I was something of a heretic amongst many colleagues. That was why I was readily perceived as being 'anti-evolution' by the creation scientists. They were so pleased when I came to southern California because they thought if Oxnard was a scientist who questioned the idea of the australopithecine fossils as human ancestors, he must be rubbishing the idea of evolution. He must therefore be in support for creation science! If only they had known!

However, this was merely my first unorthodox idea. Several other unorthodox (often even heretical) ideas have followed as I have come to investigate human structure in new ways. Many of these unorthodox ideas have given me grief, but also a great deal of intellectual enjoyment.

Chapter 2
Ideas about Sex: Yesterday, Today and Tomorrow

Relatively early in my scientific life I was involved in thinking about sex, because, following where my work led, I was trying to understand the ways in which species may be related through evolution. I knew, as did everyone, that complicating factors in such comparisons were the differences between the sexes of the same species. Though male and female are rather similar in some creatures, they are widely different in others, and this has been called sexual dimorphism. Thus, the differences between the averages for each sex in a single species can be much bigger than the difference between the averages of two species. This has led more than once to difficulties in evolutionary assessments. I tried to examine this and related differences. It is interesting to document how this interest arose.

In order to obtain funds in 1978 to support a Research Fellow (Susan Sima Lieberman), I applied for, and obtained internal university funds for a seminar to develop an undergraduate course on 'Similarities and differences between the sexes: Biological, anthropological, sociological and psychological differences'. The staff for this course, willingly co-opted from around the university, were not only Sue Lieberman and I as the biologists, but also two academics in each of other three areas: anthropology, sociology and psychology. This was occurring when more people were starting to notice new implications of sex and gender.

For the first couple of meetings, I wondered whether I had not made a terrible mistake: the meetings were so angry, everyone was talking in their own jargon, everyone was talking past everyone else, even the words sex and gender were conflated! But gradually we started to get our act together and the end result was a fascinating course, but at that point in time, we all thought, more suitable as a graduate, rather than undergraduate course. (Figures 2.1 and 2.2).

But, of course, there are many sex differences other than size. A second well known difference is in decoration (Figures 2.3 and 2.4).

And a third sex difference relates to marked complexities of reproductive mechanisms (Figures 2.5 and 2.6).

These are examples of complex reproductive differences between the sexes. In contrast, sometimes sexual dimorphism is simply described by measurements (Figure 2.7).

But it is also well-known that dimorphism is quantitatively evident in other ways (Figure 2.8). In terms of hormonal data, for example, male and female can display not only separate means but completely different spreads.

Such sexual differences may provide problems for understanding relationship and evolution. For example, when sexual dimorphism is large, then the average differences between individual specimens may be greater than the differences between the averages of whole species. This is not too much of a problem for defining living specimens and species, where we have a great deal of other biological information.

But when the specimens are fossils, or forensic, and often, therefore, incomplete, then assigning them to a species, never mind just a sex, may be compromised by such differences.

Many times, especially in paleontology, sex differences and species differences have been confused. Figure 2.9a illustrates the problem in anthropology, and Figure 2.9b the problem in forensics.

Ideas about Sex: Yesterday, Today and Tomorrow 29

Figs. 2.1. and 2.2. Two long known examples of large size sexual dimorphism.

30 *Humans and Change: Seven Ideas out of the Ordinary*

Figs. 2.3. and 2.4. Differences in decoration.

Perhaps it is also worth reminding ourselves just how much such statistics can change over time. Figure 2.10 shows plots of data from Sweden (a country that has been keeping very good records for a very long time). It shows just how much the population sex structure has changed even in just the last 150 years.

**Female very big!
May eat the male after copulation**

**Female small and like a pupa
Can't even get around**

Fig. 2.5. One species of spider has a very large female; one species of moth has a female that is wingless and becomes, essentially, just a pupa containing eggs!

This kind of information is especially problematical when specimens are incomplete, even, fragmentary (as fossils usually are), and especially when one may not know which specimens are male and which female (which may be difficult to determine). Can this be further examined?

The problem is particularly clearly shown by analysis of some tooth lengths from *Gigantopithecus* fossils (Figure 2.11).

The two left pictures of Figure 2.11 are the distributions when the data are analyzed as male and female, as defined by the paleontologists. The right hand distribution is that given by the entire data set when sexes are not defined. There is no evidence of dimorphism in this right hand distribution. The putative split into sexes in the left hand comparisons is based purely upon paleontologists defining the smaller ones as female and the larger as male (and the assumption of equal numbers of each!). This contrasts

This is the female: the male is a parasite, in the vagina of the female!

Fig. 2.6. Male is little more than a parasite. Upper frame: Just in case you think I am sexist: a female angler fish: the male is merely a parasite in the reproductive tract of the female. Lower frame: the transmutation of this information into art.

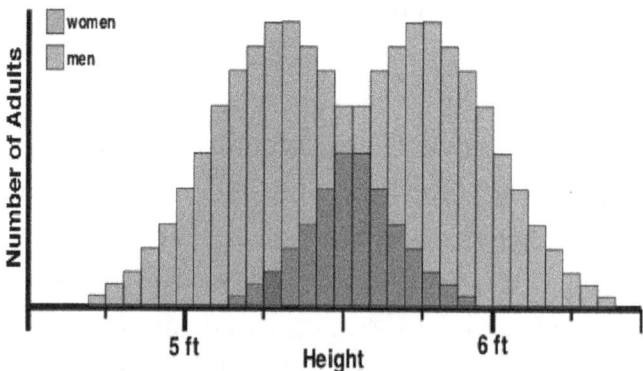

Fig. 2.7. Distribution of height in a sample of humans: approximately similar normal distributions for each sex, but staggered in their means.

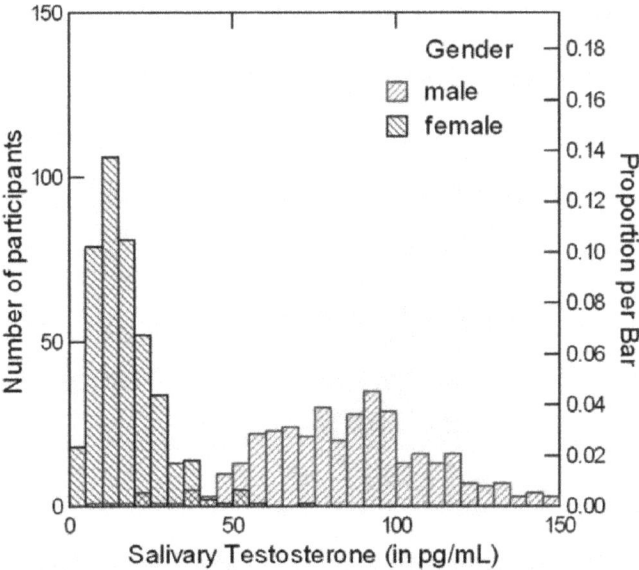

Fig. 2.8. Salivary testosterone in a sample of men and women: different means and different spreads for each sex.

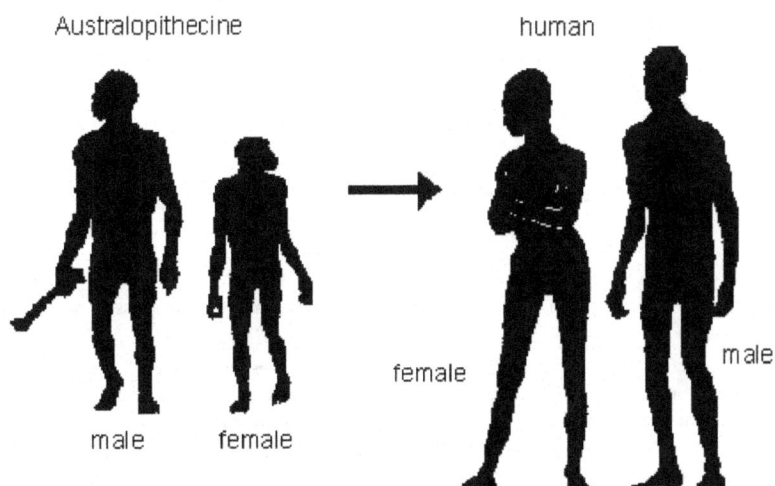

Fig. 2.9a. The differences between male and female australopithecines, though small in absolute terms, are proportionately much greater than in the much taller, but more similar male and female (and probably much better fed) Californians of today.

**Years later in the Centre for Forensic Science, <u>UWA 2000s</u>
I was lucky enough to collaborate with <u>Dan Franklin</u>
Investigating sex differences in forensic specimens**

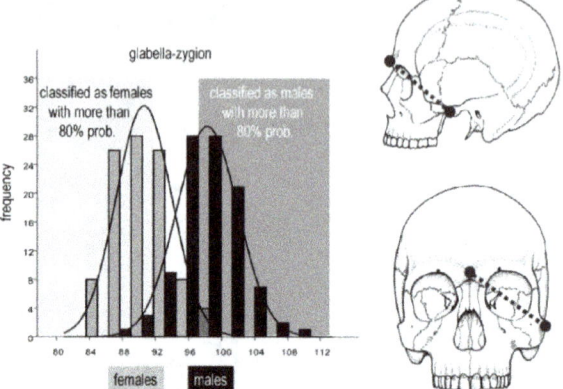

Simple one-dimensional test: strong overlap between the sexes

**However a Seven Dimensional test, much more powerful,
♂ produces almost complete separation!**

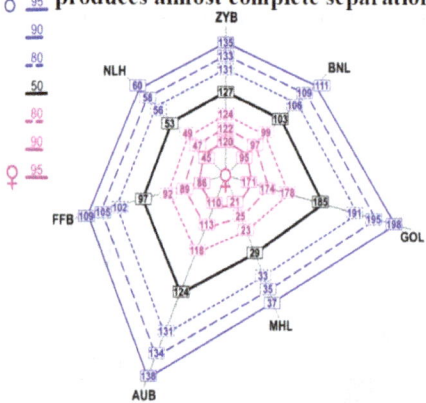

Fig. 2.9b. Differences between males and females is small when assessed by only one measurement.

Differences between males and females are small (left frame) when assessed by only one measurement shown in two views on the right. But the difference is much more distinguishable in the lower figure 2.9b when assessed by many (in this case) seven variables, each of which individually shows only a small difference.

Ideas about Sex: Yesterday, Today and Tomorrow 35

Fig. 2.10. The shape of Swedish population statistics: males black, females grey, for each year of life from birth (below) to death (above). (Data after Statistika Sweden, Kaj Talungs.)

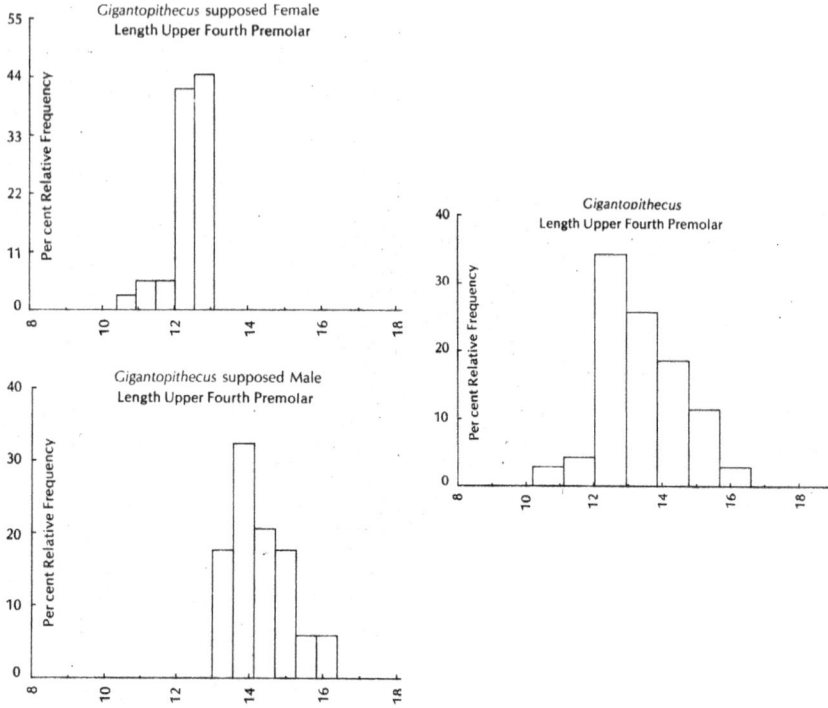

Fig. 2.11. The distribution for each purported sex for the length of the upper fourth premolar in the huge fossils from China: *Gigantopithecus*.

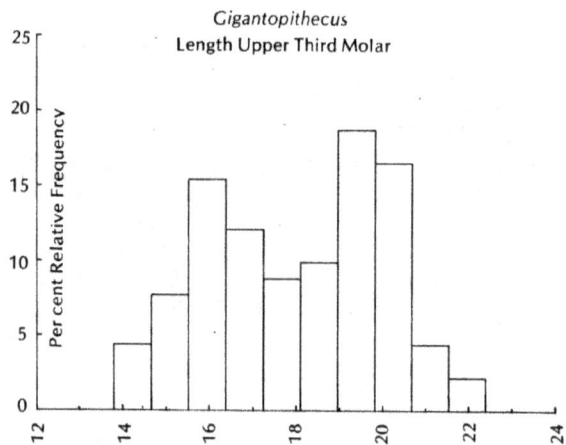

Fig. 2.12. Length of upper third molar shows a clear bimodal distribution.

Fig. 2.13. Some well-known chromosomal differences between sexes.

completely with the sex-free statistics for the length of the upper third molar for the same species (Figure 2.12).

Of course, sexual dimorphism also involves many other genetic, developmental, anatomical, physiological, behavioral, social and psychological factors (Figures 2.13, 2.14 and 2.15).

Equally, the development of human sex organs are both similar (early) and different (later) (Figure 2.15).

This makes the matter very complex to such a degree that abnormalities of development can make it very difficult to assess sex at birth.

Fig. 2.14. Speaks for itself.

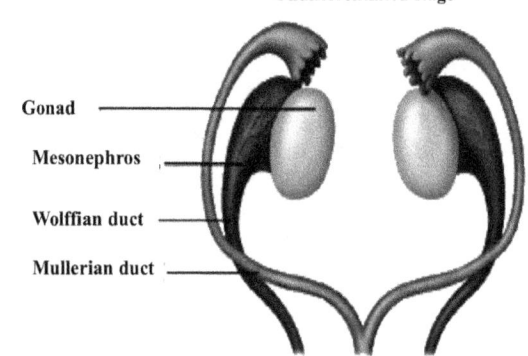

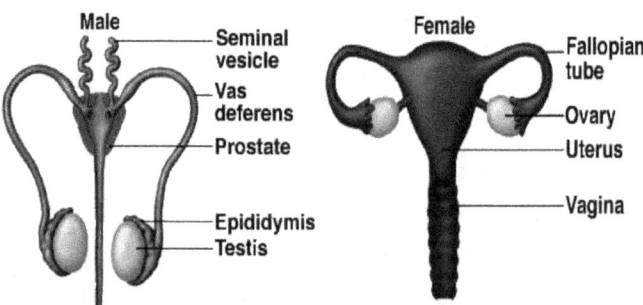

Fig. 2.15. The similarities and differences in the developmental stages of human sex organs.

Chapter 3
More on Sex: Yesterday's Changes

There are many other features of sex that are different from one species to another. For instance, some data for onset of puberty in humans at the present time are summarized in Figures 3.1 and 3.2.

But how do the average ages at puberty in humans today, of approximately twelve and fourteen years respectively, compare with those for our closest living relatives?

Some information is available about the onset of puberty (or first birth as a close guess) for some non-human primates. They all imply much shorter times to puberty and sexual maturity than humans have today. Regular chimpanzee females enter puberty about seven years, pygmy chimpanzee females at about five years. For baboons, the onset of puberty is even slightly earlier, 4–5 years. And of course, there are sex differences (Figures 3.3 and 3.4).

In rhesus monkeys the beginnings of menarche are evident at just over two years (Figure 3.5).

In humans, in contrast, the time to puberty is much greater than in non-human primates (Figures 3.6 to 3.9). Nevertheless, very good data show that in a nearly 20-year period (1991 to 2008), the times to menarche in humans have been falling (Figure 3.6).

So, what has happened to drive down the time to puberty in humans over these few years? There are many, and undoubtedly interacting, possible causes for these lower ages at menarche now

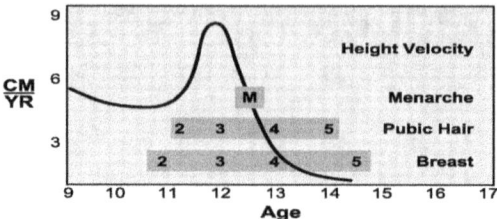
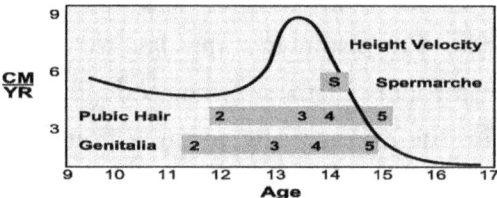

Fig. 3.1. Some differences in sexual development in girls and boys.

Fig. 3.2. Speaks for itself.

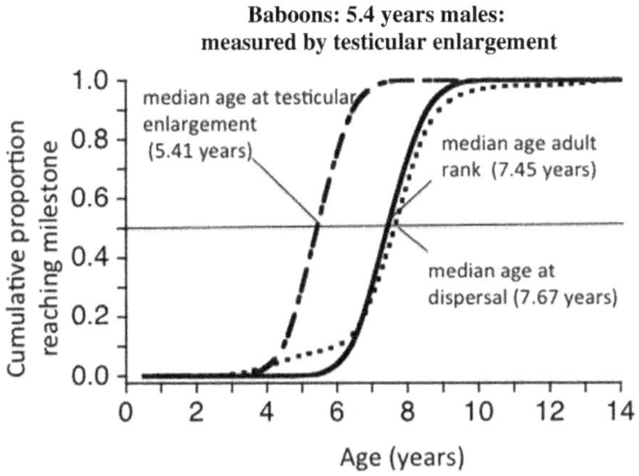

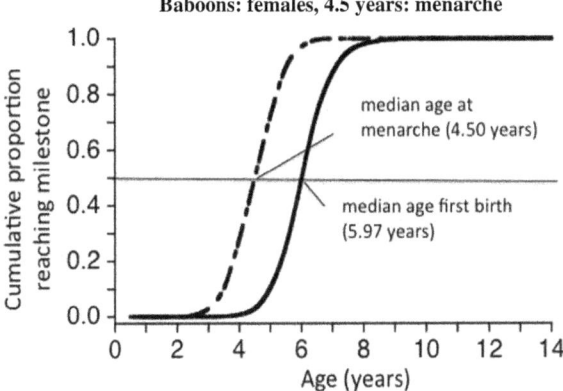

Fig. 3.3. Data for male baboons.

Fig. 3.4. Data for female baboons.

as compared with earlier times. Examples include the obvious changes: in nutrition, disease, social condition, and environment. Certainly, modern data document specifically the deleterious effects on menarche of short periods of severe malnutrition, deep economic and social depression, poor, damaging and dangerous environments, even the effects of migrant camps, prisons, wars, and so on.

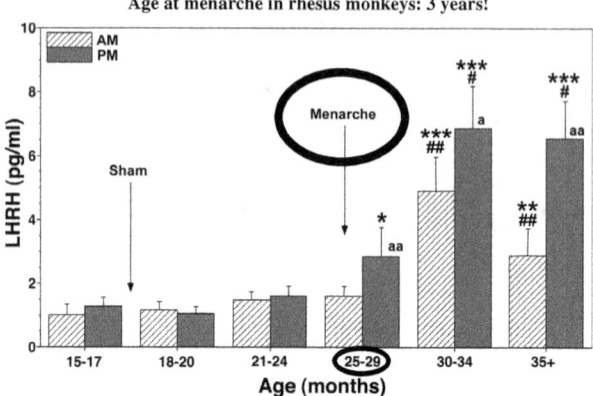

Fig. 3.5. Age at menarche in rhesus monkeys.

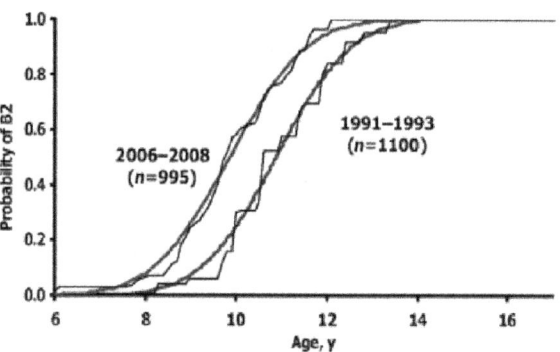

Fig. 3.6. Very good data on the reducing age at menarche in the UK over a recent near 20-year period.

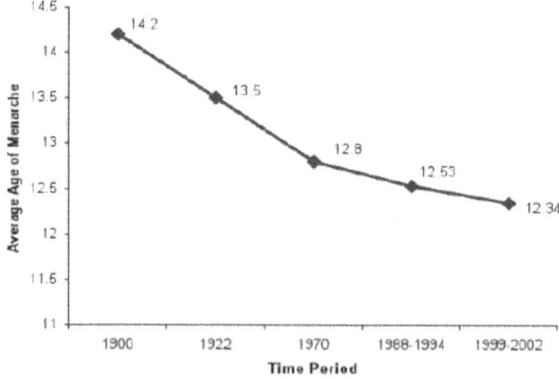

Fig. 3.7. Reasonable data from the UK showing reduction of age of menarche in the last 100 years.

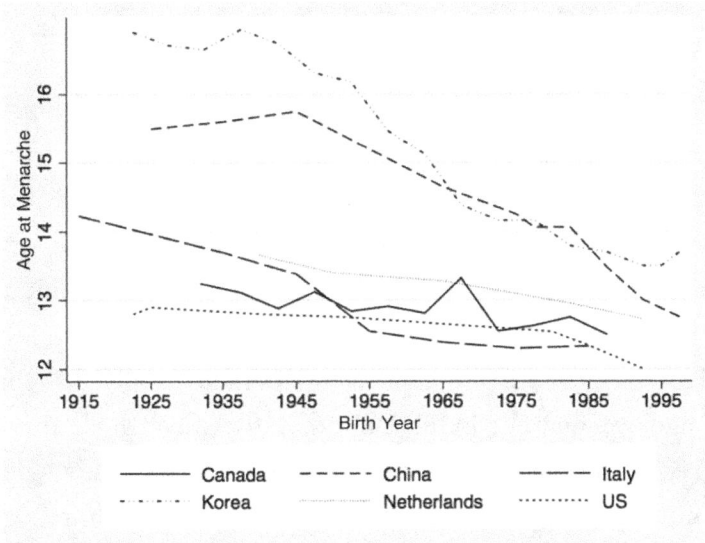

Fig. 3.8. Fair data show that this reduction is also evident internationally.

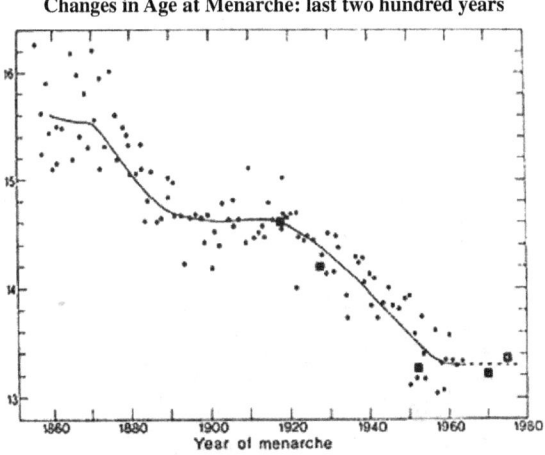

Fig. 3.9. Somewhat poor data showing a yet similar picture over an even earlier time span worldwide.

But is there a Fly in the Ointment?

Whereas the statistics for humans today say that by now, menarche, though reducing, still occurs at the beginning of the teen years, a number very high compared to monkeys and apes, there is also information about specific individuals today in whom menarche has occurred surprisingly much earlier!

Some early menarche cases have been known for a long time and are various pathological forms of precocious puberty. For example, there are, at the present time, at least six known medical conditions of this type. One of these is the McCune–Albright Syndrome, one individual with this condition was pregnant at age eight years. But, of course, such cases are special pathologies.

However, in very recent years, the statistically determined mean age of menarche in the United States (mean at about twelve years) is surrounded by well-determined spreads of values (i.e. for large normal samples). This indicates that some children (not having any of the precocious puberty syndromes) are actually entering puberty much earlier than expected.

Thus, according to the Journal of Pediatrics:

15 percent of normal American girls now enter puberty at or before age seven(!)

Even though the mean age is around 12–14. What is the evidence? Six examples are shown in Figures 3.10 to 3.15).

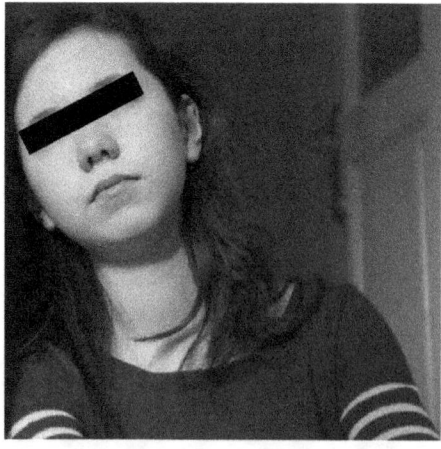

Fig. 3.10. Eight years old: pubescent.

Fig. 3.11. Seven years old: pubescent.

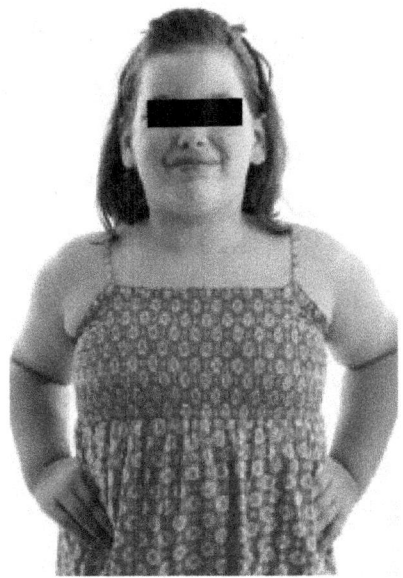

Fig. 3.12. Six years old at time of her first child.

Thus, though the mean age of menarche in humans is still considerably higher than in apes and monkeys, these data imply that in recent years in the USA, human values may possibly be reducing back towards those in non-humans.

As can be seen from the pictures, this last set of reductions occur in well-nourished normal individuals, and do not seem to

46 *Humans and Change: Seven Ideas out of the Ordinary*

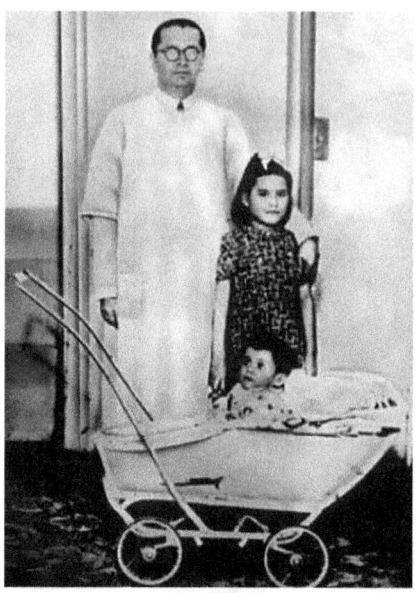

Fig. 3.13. She had her first child at five years (above), and this is mother and child three years later (below), though this case is not from the USA, and is several years ago.

be due to the negative effects of the various medical conditions mentioned before. To the degree that this latest fall has been recognized, it has been imputed by some to hormones, possibly occurring from hormonal additions or contaminations in food and water, and so on, and this may well be occurring to some degree.

More on Sex: Yesterday's Changes 47

Fig. 3.14. Five years old when she developed breasts.

But these findings also suggest a different idea. Human values may actually have started low, like those of other primates, and that may have been a very long time ago (for example, see Figure 3.16). They must then have moved higher to reach modern standards.

Four years old – and menstruating!

Fig. 3.15. Four years old and menstruating!

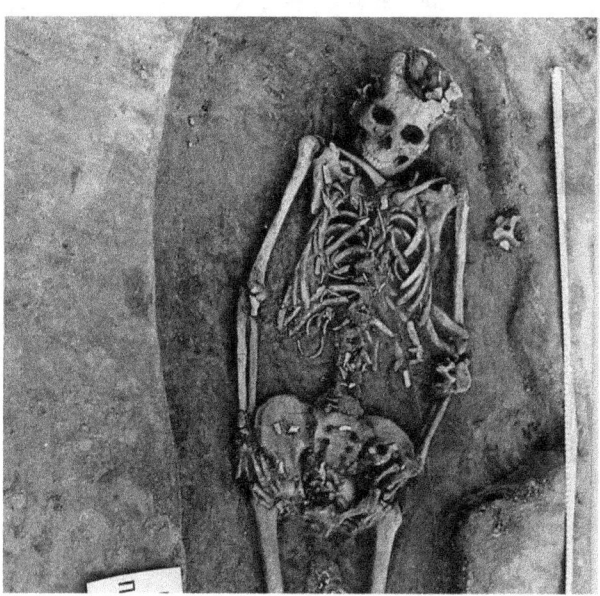

Fig. 3.16. Evidence from 7,700 years ago: 10–12-year-old died while pregnant with twins.

One figure (3.16) shows that a really low time for human menarche did occur thousands of years ago. Of course, that evidence is only from a single skeleton of the genus *Homo*. In general, it is obviously difficult to get direct information about sexual development from fossils.

But indirect information is available from comparisons of fossil skeletal data. Figures 3.17 and 3.18 suggest earlier puberty in earlier forms.

And something similar is implied by first molar eruption times of six even older non-human fossils (Figure 3.18).

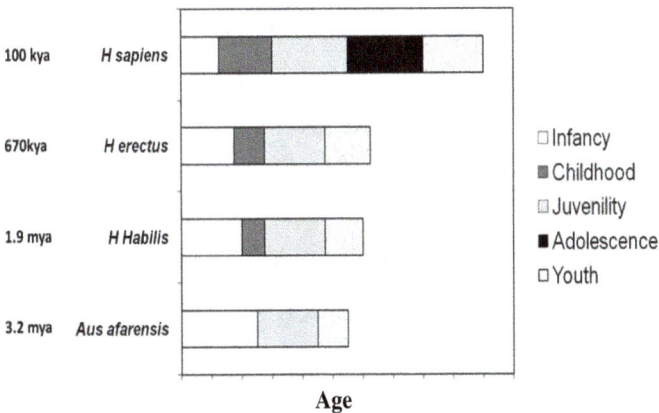

Fig. 3.17. Tooth status and development in some fossils compared with modern humans.

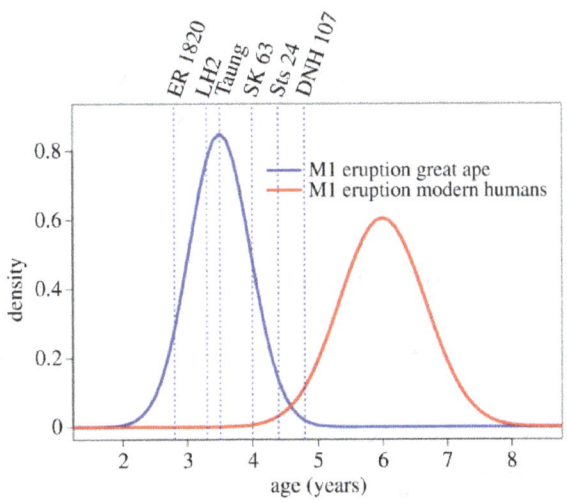

Fig. 3.18. Comparison of the curve for modern great ape and human tooth developments, compared with (dashed lines), positions of particular putative human ancestors.

Is it possible that pre-humans, very early humans, or just ancient humans, started menarche much earlier, in fact, not too different from other non-human primates?

We can think of many factors that might favor increases of time to puberty in evolving humans over the long period since then.

However, what about the recent reversals, a fall back, especially in first world nations, in the last few decades? Is this just a statistical aberration? Or could it be real, so that puberty today really is falling back, returning closer to those of the other primates? If this is even only a vague possibility, we should try to guess what those factors might be!

All this leads to a further unusual idea, expressible as other questions:

> **Are the ways apes and monkeys now, with puberty in single figures, the way pre-humans or even archaic humans were back then?**
>
> **In much earlier times, did 'something', or 'somethings' markedly delay human puberty from the 4–7 or so years of most other large primates to the eighteen and more years of humans a century ago? What might these changes have been?**
>
> **And today: has that (have those) 'something(s)' been removed, so that we are gradually reverting back to the earlier figures of non-humans, say even 4–7 years?**
>
> **Is a new non-pathological 'earlier puberty' in humans today just a return to a degree of 'normal puberty' for most higher primates?**
>
> **What could be the factor, (or factors) driving such paradoxical change? Presumably even wondering about this is just another heresy!**
>
> **But perhaps it is among the Ideas out of the Ordinary that are worth thinking about!**

Chapter 4
Ideas about Gender: Women's Struggles (and Men's)!

Questioning sex led me to look at gender. That came especially from the careers of the women I have known in science and medicine, careers that were a major struggle, often a prolonged struggle. These accounts of the **struggles of 'my' women** may be of special interest to the new generations of women who are entering, or wondering if they should enter, research, teaching, academic, even academico-political, careers today. Further, describing these struggles, leads to recognition of a new set of struggles, **struggles for men**, not parallel to those for women, but, *like Aldi,* different from!

My First Woman in Science in Birmingham: Her fight, Her Struggle

A new medical student, near the end of my very first term of teaching anatomy in medical school, asked for an appointment to see me in my office! That worried me! Appointments were not necessary. I saw the students twice a week in the human anatomy dissecting laboratory!

Her question: "Do you remember what you said at the beginning of the course?"

"What?", I queried.

"Well, if we had any problems we were to feel free to talk with you about them."

"Yeeees!", I said (with a sinking feeling).

"Weeell", she repeated, stringing me along!

"Weeeeeeell", she said, getting to the point:

"I'm pregnant!"

You can imagine what **dark things** ran through my mind! Don't forget, that was the early sixties! The only 'treatments' I knew for this 'condition' were many stiff gins, very long hot showers, horseback riding, falling downstairs, or, even yet more dangerously, a wire coat hanger in a backstreet establishment. (This was so even if some of our department's researches were, among other things, on the early contraceptives.)

But of course, she was very happy. Her pregnancy was very much wanted. We all celebrated. The **dark things** that had bubbled up in my mind evaporated. **But the real dark thing** was that she, who might have been **my first woman in science**, had her **struggle**, and left medicine!

My Second Woman in Science: At the University of Chicago

The City of Chicago had a program that permitted students from any of the Chicago Universities to take a course, *for free*, at any of the other Chicago Universities — as long as a similar course was not available in their own institution. The courses I gave were the start of my first book, and were unique to our school. So, I had students in that course from most of the other schools. I once gave a mark of ten to a student from Northwestern University in Chicago. I had never given a ten, the top mark, before.

That student was Kathy Reichs, who years later would write a series of highly successful books, TV programs, and so on. I particularly remember her first book: *Death Du Jour*, the French words being because she did her first forensic anatomy work in Canada!

Years later we were in contact again. She still remembered that ten! Chicago staff rarely gave a ten! When, many years later, I (respectfully) asked for news of her next production, she sent me, not her next book title (authors usually hide a forthcoming title), but a photograph of her grandchild! She, too, had a **struggle**, but a **highly successful struggle**.

My Third Woman in Science was Betty Jean

She did a marvelous thesis, and obtained a top PhD that won her the All-American Hrdlička Prize. But **her struggle** became especially evident when she started looking for postdoctoral jobs. She (anatomy, anthropology) and her partner (accountancy, business), naturally wanted jobs in the same city, but their disciplines ran on different calendars. One would get an offer, the other would be turned down. And *vice versa* through several cycles. They were getting desperate. I even wrote to selection committees trying to pull rank as dean; but it did no good, none of them would help, none of them were willing to allow concurrent decisions! So, she gave up research, **her struggle**!

It was, eventually, all good however. She did another degree, medicine, in the same city as her husband, and is now a very high level radiologist. **Stupid academia lost out**.

My Fourth Woman in Science was a 'Pushy Freshman' (sic)

In Chicago, helped by Mrs. Loeb of Astor Street, Chicago, I had been able to organize a program of summer research for third year undergraduates. One student, Rebecca, wanted to do it with me, and in the summer at the end of her FIRST year! Why me? And why as early as first year?

Well, this 'Freshman' was a bit of a math prodigy and wanted to use her mathematics in biology. So, I agreed. First student I ever had whom I did not have to send away to learn matrix algebra! At sixteen(!) she already knew it, or learnt it quickly, I never knew which! (The University of Chicago would take suitably qualified people whatever their age.)

Of course, she was only a first year, but she had heard about the program from a senior student (in Hillel: Foundation for Jewish Campus Life), and SHE wanted it NOW. She and I thoroughly enjoyed that experience. She continued research with me in each summer of two more undergraduate years. We published papers together. I took her to speak at a symposium in Antananarivo, Madagascar (we were working on Malgache primates). She went on to a Masters with David Raup at Rochester, and a Doctorate with Steve Gould at Harvard. What a chance for an undergraduate! This sounds like she had no struggle.

In fact, however, unbeknownst to me, she **was** touched by **the struggle**. Years later, during a research visit to Australia on a prestigious Fulbright Fellowship, she told me that, in her early postgraduate years at Harvard, she had been asked a question: **Was Oxnard good in bed?!** It was assumed by her colleague that this was how she did it. **Her struggle: ARRGGGHHHH!**

My Fifth Woman in Science

A high school student in Los Angeles, in 1979, was not really my student, but the daughter of one of my secretarial assistants, Nancy. Nancy wanted to know if I would talk with her teenage daughter, Julia. Nancy's (and therefore Julia's) family name was Figueroa, and that says much in California! None of their family had ever gone to university. But, said Nancy, Julia seemed very bright, and would I talk with her? Of course, I agreed.

Julia came, and during our talk I showed her some reprints of my scientific papers. At the end, when she was about to go, Julia asked if I would give her one of those papers. "I'll do more than that," I said, "I'll give you a whole book." And I gave her my then most recent book: **The Order of Man**. (The feminists on campus had agreed to my using this title, the word **'Man'** being the English translation of the word **Homo**, the genus in the zoological **Order** to which we all belong.) Julia asked me to write in it. So, I wrote:

> *"These are the Voyages of the Star Ship **Julia**,*
> *to Boldly go, where no Man, **or Woman,** has gone before!"*

That was in the early days of Star Trek, when they still had their original statement: "Where No **Man** Has Gone Before". Nowadays, of course, a masculine Captain Kirk has mutated into female captains as tough as Garrett, as ambitious as Shelby, as likeable as Jadzia, and as interestingly flawed as Janeway.

Years after, on a return visit to southern California, I ran into Nancy on campus. She told me how much that talk had meant to Julia, that Julia still had the book, that she had indeed gone on to university, the first in her family, qualified in pharmacy, and become a successful practitioner **(another woman in science, and her successful struggle!)**. Wow! The Wonders of Teaching! Do we really ever know what our words can mean to students?

My Sixth Woman in Science

One particularly interesting **struggle** only came to light when Eleanor and I were guests at the Konrad Lorenz Institute many years later. It was a small, exclusive, high-level symposium attended by only a handful of academics and a few very lucky local students. We had a whole session each for our presentations, and plenty of time to hammer out problems with discussion.

At breakfast, on that first morning, Eleanor and I, always early for food, met one of the other speakers, Deidre McCloskey, also early. The usual questions ensued: "What was your school?" For her, the University of Chicago. "Oh, when?", I asked. For her, in the late sixties. "Oh, I don't remember you", I said, (reminding her that I was her dean at the time). She then reminded me I was chair of the committee that interviewed her! Still no memory!

Then she told us she had since taken gender reassignment. I had indeed chaired the committee that had interviewed and appointed **him**.

How had it all been, we gently asked? Oh, she said, absolutely the best decision I could have made. And she gave me her then latest book about the very kinds of statistics that I was using. That book, published in 2008, with Stephen Ziliak, was entitled: *The Cult of Statistical Significance*. It is a marvelous book, pointing out that, however important many of the earlier statistics were in the social, life and medical sciences, they were also capable of being mishandled.

Thus, she had a yet **different kind of struggle** — but has been highly successful.

Famous Women in Science: Their Famous Struggles!

I have also been fortunate enough to know about, even, sometimes, to actually know, a number of truly famous women scientists.

The Lady with the Pie Chart

Fig. 4.1. Florence Nightingale and one of her pie charts.

The first was Florence Nightingale. Of course, I never knew her in the flesh, I am not *that* old. But early in secondary school, I was set to write an essay on her life at a time when I was wondering where I might go. I was fascinated by her story, **by her struggle**. She was the Lady with the Pie Chart (Figure 4.1). Her behavior was said to be exasperating and eccentric, and she had no respect for upper-class British women. She even said:

*"If given a choice between being woman or slave,
then I would choose the freedom of a slave"!*

Her struggle: in carrying out her work she was stymied by hospital teams (men), by army officers (men), and by London government officialdom (men).

So, she produced many statistical pie charts to make her case. She got the ear of the Secretary for War, Sidney Herbert. She reduced mortality in the army from 42 percent to 2 percent by simple things: better food, washing hands, scrubbing brushes,

Fig. 4.2. Dorothy Crowfoot Hodgkin.

removing dirty clothes, and, *especially, training nurses and trying to 'train' doctors*!

She was the first woman to receive the Order of Merit, an award that, by its definition, could only be held by 24 Living English **Men**.

The next female living English **Man** (Figure 4.2) got the Order of Merit 50 years later.

Dorothy also received the Nobel Prize (Figure 4.3) in 1964, for determining the structures, by early X-ray crystallography, of three special molecules: penicillin, cyanocobalamin (vitamin B12) and insulin. I knew her because I worked on vitamin B12 in those early years.

I have my story about her. I was, very early, elected to the Zoo Club (a Scientific Dining Society at Regents Park). Outside speakers to the Zoological Society of London would be invited to dine at the Zoo Club afterwards. The day that Dorothy was the speaker there was consternation. There were then no women in the Zoo Club.

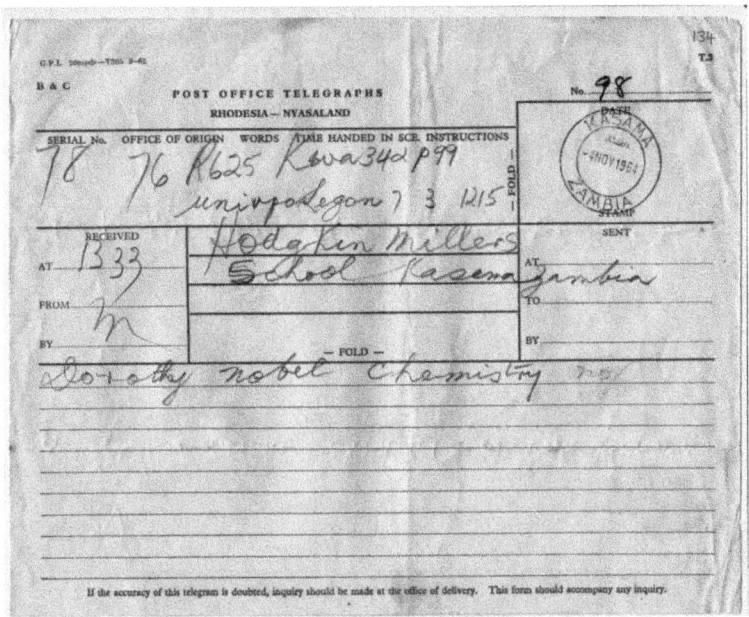

Fig. 4.3. This is how they told you about a Nobel in those days!

So, she was invited to dine with a member of the secretarial staff behind a curtain! Wow! Her Struggle!

Did she tell them where to go!

I think the rules were changed at the next meeting!

Barbara McClintock (Figure 4.4) was the first woman to win the Nobel Prize unshared. But her **first struggle, her first battle,** was: **The Battle of Luke and Longnose** (Figure 4.5).

In fact, however, as a scientist working on corn genetics, she discovered 'mobile genetic elements' (better known as 'jumping genes', Figure 4.6).

Her **struggle** was with her male antagonists. Sewall Wright, founder of population genetics, said she did not understand the underlying mathematics. Top molecular biologist Joshua Lederberg said "By God, that woman is crazy". And most other genet-

Fig. 4.4. A young Barbara.

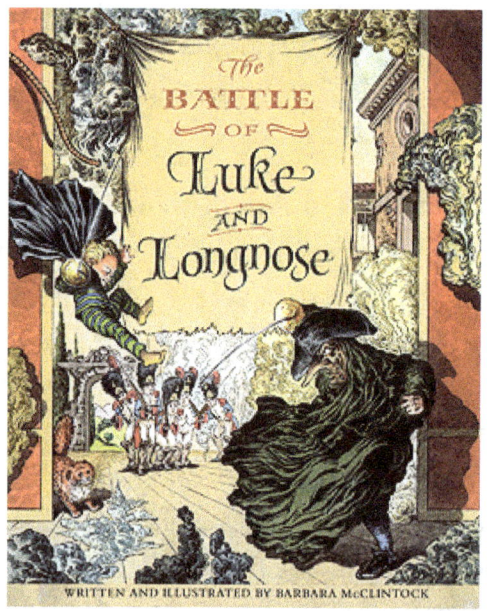

Fig. 4.5. The 'Battle' in one of her books.

icists (all males) said she was just plain wrong. She felt she had crossed a desert alone; no-one had followed her.

But George Beadle (a prior Nobel Prize winner himself) encouraged her and helped her career. (Beadle was President of

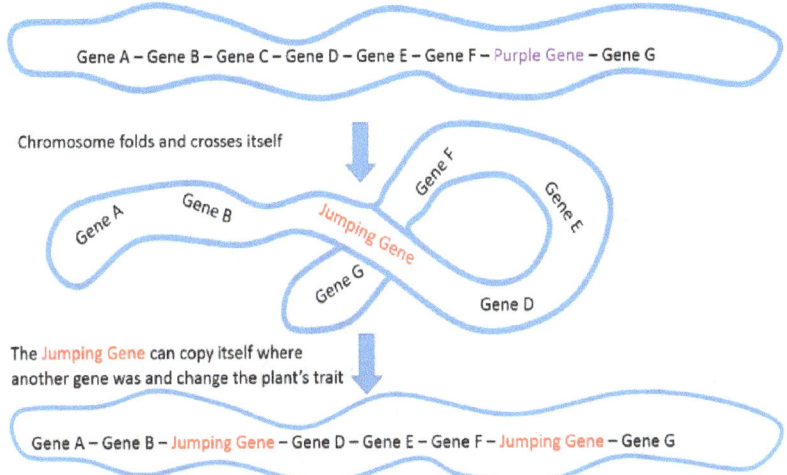

Fig. 4.6. The concept of the jumping gene.

Fig. 4.7. A later Barbara McClintock.

The University of Chicago during my time there.) Very much later, she was honored with her face on a USA postage stamp (Figure 4.7).

Another scientist (H. K. Markey: a name not well known as a scientist to most of us) was, in fact, a mathematician (Figure 4.8). But she was also into art and music.

One of her 'colleagues' was Victor Mature!

Fig. 4.8. H. K. Markey, also an actress, and one of her roles as Catwoman.

She applied her knowledge of the long rolls of paper, with 88 rows of perforations in various positions to produce music in player pianos, to inventing a way to use them for frequency hopping to control a torpedo (1942, Figure 4.9).

Admiral Dönitz was perplexed at the sudden increase in U-boat kills!

Interestingly, a number of MEN tried to prove that she didn't do this, that she piggy-backed onto the work the by her male collaborators! That was not true.

But it was part of **her struggle**!

Where have all the Young Men Gone? Leaving Town, One by One!

One of the first appointments I made when I arrived at the University of Western Australia (department heads had those powers in those days) was Nina Jablonski.

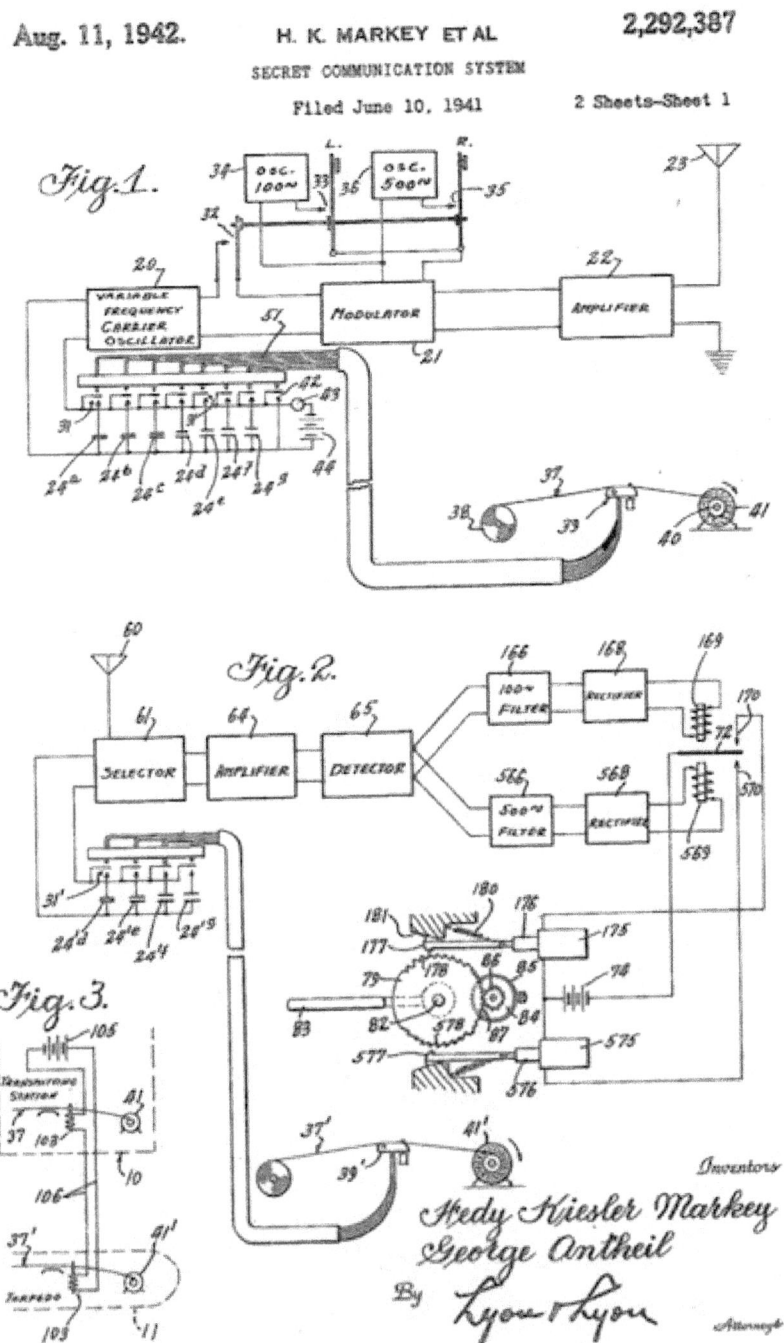

Fig. 4.9. A drawing of her invention, signed Hedy Kiesler Markey (*aka* **Hedy Lamarr**, in case you haven't got it!).

I told Nina the story of my beginning research grant applications in Australia. I had been successful with external grants. But my internal grant applications to UWA had failed.

Nina smiled, gently:

"Oh" she said,
"Just delete the word evolution from your grant titles!".

She had learnt this from the Women's Group on campus, an organization to which I, of course, did not have access. The next year proved her right. Success!

But in our more detailed discussions, Nina wanted to know what we could do about another problem: not so much about supporting women (of course we were already doing that — I had supported her), but we were also recognizing a developing reverse problem for men!

We studied the statistics of the matter in various countries, but the results can be best mirrored in just two recent numbers from our own school at UWA: in 2015, we had **just six male, but thirty-three female research students**!!!

Nina and I both wanted to know: was university education going to become primarily for women? Were men being driven into jobs not requiring a university education? And what would happen if this process spread more widely through our society? This is almost the opposite of what is currently happening in some countries in the Middle East!

Part of the reason for our interest in this problem stemmed from the fact that we were both (separately) carrying out research in China. I started earlier with Hong Kong colleagues, during visits not long after the end of the Cultural Revolution.

Nina started rather later, she is much younger, but she had held an appointment in Hong Kong for several years. We had both been in China several times, and once or twice, even, together. I had known her doctoral supervisor in the USA.

As a result, we both were starting to see the effects of the one-child policy in China, stemming from Mao's time. Fewer young people were supporting many old! And there were fewer women than men (Figure 4.10).

As a result of that one-child policy, however, changes were already occurring in China.

One was an effect on males. It was producing *Guang gun* (光棍: bare branches — men with no wives). Wonderfully poetic descriptions the Chinese have!

A second effect was on females. It was producing *Sheng nu* (剩女: leftover women — women with no husbands). Again, a picturesque description.

There is normally, in China, much pressure from family, friends and the State for women to marry. But, in China, women

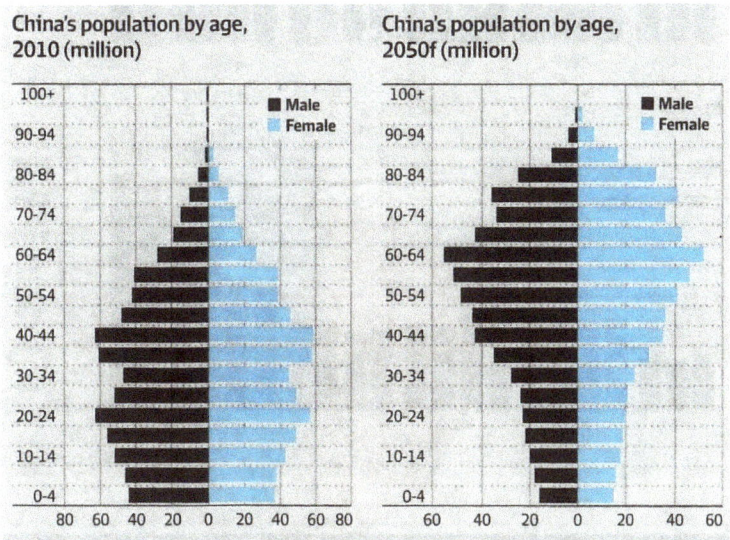

Fig. 4.10. China's population by sex and age in 2010 (left), and estimated for 2050 (right).

tend to 'marry up', men to 'marry down'. If you are 'Sheng Nu', you are top quality and therefore there are no 'topper-quality' men for you!

Figure 4.11 shows one of the causes of these effects: abortion rates.

In China, such figures were partly due to abortions after a first (and only, therefore) child, a policy that favored male conceptus products over female. Could this, in the longer term, produce debilitating social changes: increased vulnerability of girls, women trafficking, pornography, prostitution, pedophilia, and female beating? Was it even leading to forced abortions, forced infanticide and forced sterilizations, possibly even forced surrogacy, and forced genetic modification and cloning techniques? There is some evidence that these things have occurred widely in China, and, perhaps, not just in the 're-education' camps.

These sex imbalances are not limited to China. Sex imbalances of various kinds, and through various mechanisms, occur in many

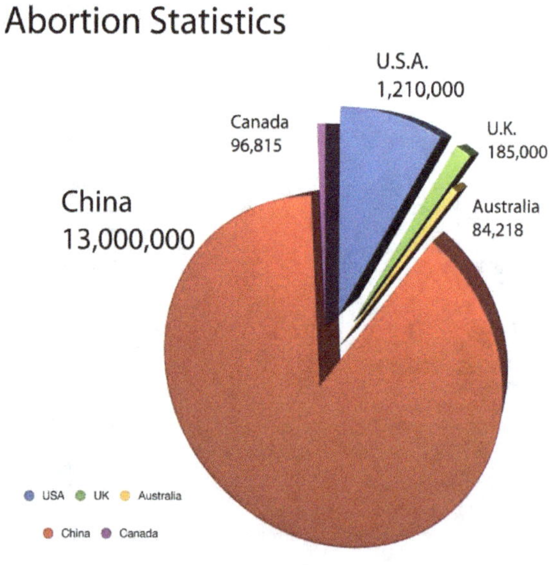
Abortion Statistics
U.S.A.
1,210,000
Canada
96,815
U.K.
185,000
China
13,000,000
Australia
84,218
USA
UK
Australia
China
Canada

Fig. 4.11. Some international abortion statistics.

other societies: in Southeast Asia, in the Indian sub-continent, in the Middle East, in Africa, indeed, almost everywhere!

Japan is such a case in reverse. In Japan, there are Hikikomori boys and Otaku men. In 2010, there were at least a million boys and young men who had withdrawn from Japanese society, living in their bedrooms, not going to school or work, kept by their parents, **unmarriageable**. Hikikomori boys (hikikomori meaning 'pulling inward' or 'shut in', 引きこもり) refuse school and spend their time playing electronic media games in their bedrooms. Otaku (meaning 'nerd', or 'geek', オタク) men play with 'Barbie' type dolls! (Indeed, one kidnapped child in Australia was kept happy during her ordeal because she had access to several Barbie-like dolls belonging to her kidnapper! Whether this was a related phenomenon, I don't know!) (Figures 4.12 to 4.14.)

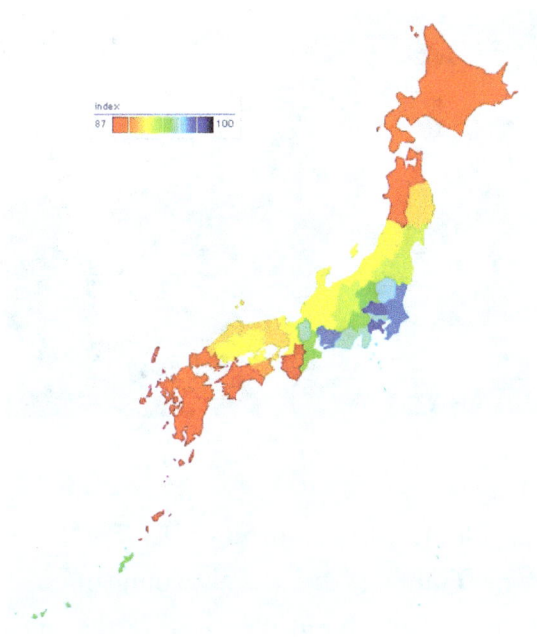

Fig. 4.12. Sex imbalance in different regions of Japan: 87/100 red to 100/100 **black**.

Fig. 4.13. Hikikomori boy!

Fig. 4.14. Otaku men!

Similar problems exist in Europe. NEETs (**N**ot in **E**ducation, **E**mployment or **T**raining) are largely young men. Such unemployed, unwanted young men, more easily than young women, drop out, become gang members, criminals, terrorists, and com-

Fig. 4.15. *The Groves of Academe*: "The End of Men".

mit sex crimes! Could all this lead to disruption of society? The matter has even reached The Atlantic (Figure 4.15).

Yet Great Things Sometimes Happen!

When I became graduate dean at the University of Southern California, one of the first things I had to do was to appoint an associate graduate dean. Obviously, this was a very important appointment, not only personally for me, but also, in general, for the graduate school, and, indeed, the entire university. We had a list of good applicants. We had a good advisory search committee. But the decision was mine (in those days — not today, I imagine!).

It was an interesting matter. I have scientific, medical (even if then non-practicing), and engineering qualifications, and the university might have expected that I would want another scientist — and we had some good candidates. At that point, this was especially important because the university was strongly boosting its science, technology, engineering and medical areas. Zohrab Kaprelian, our provost, was a most enterprising engineer, and with the California Institute of Technology just down the road in Pasadena, he did not try to compete, but went in different, non-competing, applied directions.

Because of this picture, however, I felt that it might be rather important that, if the dean and the provost were both in scientific and technical areas, perhaps the new assistant (later associate) dean of the graduate school should come from some other, quite different, discipline. And it happened that we had a very good candidate (in my opinion) who was from the general area of the humanities! Indeed, **his** doctoral thesis (1973) was on The Poetic Language of Aimé Césaire! This was totally new to me. But I was intrigued. I was persuaded that **he** would be the best appointment.

At this point, I realized that there were mutterings in the dovecotes. Why had Oxnard, with scientific, medical and engineering qualifications, picked someone from the **humanities**? But that was not all.

Why had Oxnard chosen a **woman**? (Because though I used the words '**his** thesis', '**his** appointment', that was merely a literary trick to hide **her** sex up to this point!)

And there was even more. Why had Oxnard picked someone who was **black**?

> *Of course, I am talking about* **Ruth Simmons**. *She came to us.*
> *We took her.*
> *And she proved* **Absolutely Superb**!

Some years later, Ruth and I had a discussion about her next career possibilities. I suggested that, from being associate dean with us, she should move to a top administrative appointment in a major university on the east coast. I even predicted to her that she would eventually become president of a very good liberal arts college.

Everyone knows what happened next. She indeed went on to a major administrative position at Princeton, and then on as president of Smith College (a top liberal arts college, following, as it happens, a prior Australian president). *And Ruth remembered my forecast at her inauguration* at Smith.

It was at this point that my forecasting failed. I did not foresee her eventual appointment as president of a major university: Brown! Nor did I foresee that, even in retirement, she would continue to be a president, this time leading Prairie View University, a public, historically black, community university.

We have remained in sporadic contact over the years. Eleanor and I were invited to her inauguration as president of Smith, later to her inauguration as president at Brown, and then, to her retirement celebrations from Brown. It was evident to both Eleanor and I just how good she had been for helping solve some of the big problems those institutions had!

And now Ruth applies herself to new challenges post retirement (something I failed to do, see last chapter).

She says:

"When I took on this challenge, I did not know that my country would experience social and political upheavals unlike any I had seen in my previous leadership roles. I did not know that a historic flood would affect the community so grievously. I did not anticipate a pandemic that would upend the way we work and experience the educational environment. I did not imagine that I would feel so grateful to be able to lead the institution through this series of challenges. I did not foresee, but hoped, that it would emerge stronger after such a perilous period, gaining in resources and reputation."

Until now, few of us have seen such incredible challenges in the work that we do!

It was always evident to Ruth that there must be new leaders assuming responsibility for advancing education to new levels of excellence in student outcomes, faculty achievements and research outputs.

What a wonderful outcome this has all been for her. And what a wonderful outcome for me, as I have made the lesser moves from mentee, to mentor, to retiree. And what a wonderful story of what should be the proper relationships amongst students and staffs in universities. Can such stories continue today? I wonder. I worry. And you should too (see last chapter).

Implications for Higher Education in the West

All these and other changes are now very serious for higher education! Reduction of resources in universities (in the West) are leading to:

The replacement of full-time teachers by part-time teachers and teaching assistants.

This is: *the casualization of the teaching staff.*

It is allied with the loss of careers and the disappearance of security for researchers.

This is: *the 'insecuritization' of the research staff.*

It has hidden administrative increases by using academic titles for many administrators.

This is *the 'pseudo-academicization' of administrators.*

Worst of all are the implications for students, hidden from teachers behind computer screens.

This is *the 'invisibility' of students*.

All this also leads to the creation of a new problem. Temporary, part-time, poorly paid, insecure jobs are of some value to those women who can, and will, undertake them, to cope with a family at the same time. They are almost useless **to all ambitious women** wanting full-time careers (with or without families). Though more temporary appointments increase the number of women in academia, an apparently desirable result, the actual effect is negative: downgrading of positions for both women and men.

Chapter 5

Dangerous Differences: Race and Ethnicity, Kindred and Ancestors

The nearly eight billion people who inhabit the Earth all belong to one species of human that we label '*Homo sapiens*', in English: 'wise human'. But many humans believe that we comprise large numbers of *separate* races, or ethnicities, or tribes, or belong to *specific* language groups, or social communities, or religions, or lands, or nations, or even just for long periods, and so on.

Many people think these categories seem Separate!
Some people think: Very Separate!
Some people even think: some Separatenesses better than Others!

Joining, Separating, Migrating, Warring, Hating!

Of course, as a biological species we are very different from most other mammals, the species of which comprise much smaller local populations, sometimes subspecies, even sometimes with hybrids, and which live in far more restricted areas, with fewer chances of successful interbreeding, and with such interbreeding as occurs often being sterile.

Yet all humans of today, and the fewer but still numerous (though less widespread) humans of earlier times, are now, and were then, highly successfully interbreedable. As a result, humans as a species differ from most non-human species of mammals, not only in their enormously increasing numbers from originally smaller populations, but also in their enormous propensity for genetic interchange. This has gone beyond local populations, across to neighboring populations, even into many apparently separate populations, through abilities to migrate, not only seasonally (common in other animals), but over long periods, over long distances, across rivers, lakes, seas, and even oceans, indeed to new lands and even between continents, and much of this in relatively very short periods of time.

This has become ever more evident from new knowledge of genes in humans. Many (possibly most) humans today share genes from the fossil ancestors of yesteryear. A quite large three percent to as much as eight percent of our genomes include genes from those older fossil groups that have so far been discovered. This is true for all of today's humans, whether from Africa, Eurasia, the Americas, even Australia.

Further, the story is not by any means complete. Future discoveries are certainly going to increase recognition of our genetic admixtures to greater and greater degrees.

Even just today, genes from four other ancient human groups are known in present day Southeast Asia and Africa! Even indigenous Australians, a group that generally thinks of itself as the world's oldest and most separate living group, contains (like the rest of us) genes of Neanderthals and Denisovans, together with those of at least one other (at present) unidentified older group. Will not more of these be discovered among most present-day human populations? Will not genetic remnants of many different 'proto-Neanderthals', 'pre-Neanderthals', 'migrant Neanderthals', 'ancient humans', and 'past migrant humans', as well as older modern humans be found in most of today's modern humans? A Nobel prize has recently been awarded for this type of work.

Notwithstanding all this human admixture, there is nothing bad, in fact it is good, to be *proud* of our own relatives, our own social groups, our own languages, our own

religions, and so on. What is bad is *hating* the relatives of others, *hating* other's social groups, other's languages, other's religions, and so on. **Why do so many of us persist in not only spuriously emphasizing 'sharp human separations', but, what is more, using them for separating from, and detracting about, and often, as a result, *'hating, hurting and even killing'* other humans?**

Such differences are described in many different ways. Skin color and facial form are the least of it. They are also defined by upstream to downstream water rights, through land rights, across sea rights, from landowners through renters to squatters, from rich through intermediate to poor, across left, center and right political groups, from democratic to autocratic rulers, among many strictly applied and very different religions, between the antagonisms of factions, the battles of tribes, the wars of nations, even the tortures and killings of homicidal and genocidal maniacs! And all of these desires for Our Separatisms, and the downgrading of Other's Separates, seem to have become especially hardened at the present time.

Why do so many of us persist in accepting such sharpnesses in human separations,
'such ethnicities', 'such races', such 'outsiders'?
Why indeed?

The earliest humans (I am sure even earlier pre-humans) looked for their next meal that same day: gathering from the earth outside the cave, scavenging, hunting and fishing more widely from local lands and waters. They picked fruits, seeds, leaves and roots for today, but also stored them, eventually growing them, for tomorrow (no preservatives in those days!). They had not only to catch and kill animals for today, but also, to hold, salt or pickle, or even keep them alive, for tomorrow (no refrigerators in those days!).

Such activities and abilities must have led to the cooperation of family members in cave and hut and tent, and thence to links with related families in hamlet and village. These, in turn, may have produced specializations (not everyone able to gather, scavenge, hunt, prepare or cook), and therefore forming dependencies upon each other's individual abilities. From the cave, hut and tent, the hamlet and village, this led to towns and cities, with increasing specializations and increasing populations.

In the cave and the hamlet, most breeding would largely be with close relatives. In the village and small town, wider breeding would widen gene pools somewhat. In the city, gene pools would become both wide and deep. Such mixing was a new phenomenon, a human phenomenon, of increasing sexual, and therefore, also social contacts.

This would also mean specializations, and specializations mean sharing and swapping, both products and ideas. The whole thing is trade! Trade leads to travel. Travel and trade lead to meetings with groups beyond the family of the cave and tent, and the related families of the hamlet and village. This is the beginnings of barter and borrowing, sharing and trust, and, with them, yet wider interbreeding.

Thus, the travelling salesperson carries genes outwards to new families, as well as new foods for them. The travelling salesperson brings back a new partner carrying new genes inwards, as well as new kind of implements. All this modifies family gene pools, both old and new, with genetic exchanges. It is not a process that occurs to any degree in animals (and in particular is quite different from seasonal migrations of animal troops, flocks or shoals).

And there are further extensions. Travel and trade do not always just mean barter and trust. Contact with wider and wider externals can lead to skepticism, perhaps suspicion and jealousy, even anger and antagonism. It can change relationships so that barter or gifts may lead to copying and stealing. Good friends can change, through suspicious competition, to hostile enemies. From travel and migration, this can become invasion, plunder, battle, war, and even genocide.

And these last extensions are a special two-way street for genetic alterations. Invaders take with them camp followers, and when successful, bring back war captives. Camp followers in the new place, and war captives once back in the old place, are of both sexes. Captured camp followers (the losses of war) modify the gene pools of enemies. War captives (the spoils of war) modify the gene pools of friends. There is then yet further and more complex mixing of gene pools. All these are mixings that scarcely occur in animals. And they are especially different from the hybrid zones at the edges of animal groups, or in seasonal animal migrations.

Finally, all these changes in gene populations, spurred on by ever increasing population sizes, lead to a larger and larger citizenry, to bigger and bigger armies. They result in movements not only between hamlets and villages over small distances, but to towns, to cities, even to city states, to even larger principalities over even larger distances. All affect both local and overall population gene pools.

And this does not occur over just a matter of a single battle, a single campaign season, a few years of war or even a few decades of hostility, but over lifetimes, generations, centuries, millennia, and even more. The propensities and abilities of humans to share genes in these ways are completely foreign to any other mammal. They account for the complex mixtures of DNA found in almost all human groups today, including admixtures stemming from their migrations of yesteryear. Even in very ancient times, such migrations encompassed whole land masses, crossed major waterways, even trespassed over continents, and did these things repeatedly. Phenomena like these produce molecular relationships among humans that are unique. Do the various data support these ideas? Do these various ideas stem from these data? Or am I just getting old?

Across the Generations: New Ideas About Ancestry

Many fossil species, almost all believed to have been involved in the evolution of today's humans, have now been named. They range from *Sahelanthropus* and *Orrorin*, perhaps ten to six million years ago, through *Ardipithecus* at say six to four million years ago, through various *Australopithecus* at say four to two million years ago, to twelve (at last count) fossil *Homo* species (including *erectus* and *neanderthalensis*) at say two million years ago and less. Modern *Homo sapiens*, ourselves, are thought to be from these older *Homo* groups.

The precise times and evolutionary relationships among these named fossils differ somewhat among different paleontologists, depending upon how they are assessed. But in general, they are almost all thought to lead (almost inexorably, one might say) to modern humans. Even the various forms of robust *Australopithecus* (originally also believed to be human ancestors, though now usually placed on sidelines at around four to two million years), are still, by many workers, believed to be closely related to modern humans. They are usually said to be only slightly offset from the main human lineage.

Of course, most of the fossils cannot tell us what *did* happen. The best they can do is suggest, possibly, what *may have* happened. And sometimes they may suggest what it is likely *might not* have happened. So, it's all a bit chancy!

But you would think that, pending very lucky evidence, we should expect:

1) many lineages to lead **only** to extinct dead ends
2) many lines to **join** as well as separate
3) many hybrids and subspecies to have both **appeared and disappeared**
4) some lines at least surely **not leading** to modern humans at all, and
5) **many migrations**, not few, along rivers within mainlands, across lakes and seas, and between continents.

Such multiple ideas are contrary to the conventional wisdom, which tends to see simple lineages, and few migrations. Perhaps, however, such ideas are starting to be suggested and tested by new studies.

First: today's paleontological investigations see so many more fossils that it is highly likely that they actually do lie in complex spreading 'bushes', or in complicated interacting 'reticulations', rather than on a few simple 'sprigs', and certainly not on any simple 'forked branch', or single 'twig'.

Second: today's functional studies of fossil anatomies are suggesting more complex behavioral possibilities. For instance, in non-human primates, there is much evidence that ground running, tree climbing, arm swinging and arm hanging, hind-limb leaping and even hind-limb hanging, each evolved separately many times. We can, therefore, also expect that two legged walking and running, the related hunting and gathering, perhaps even the multiple migrating, may well also have evolved more than once. New evidence seems to show that this is particularly true of walking and running on two legs, even though many workers seem to assume this was a unique occurrence. There may even have evolved movement patterns not existing at all today (see next paragraph!).

Third: today's studies also negate the simple idea that human evolution occurred on relatively treeless plains, looking mainly to other terrestrial species as models. Such studies tend to eschew most other environmental possibilities (such as, for instance, forested environments trailing off into close savannah, mountain and valley environments with marked environmental differences, and waterside environments in which mixed environments are present, for example: the riverbank, the swamp, the beach, the delta, and the archipelago).

Fourth: today's modelling studies (see below) imply that migrations have been very numerous and very complex, negating the idea of only one or just very few major migrations.

Fifth, and most importantly: today's molecular data, both data that can sometimes be obtained from the fossils, but especially comparative data from the living, imply complicated genetic interrelationships rather than simple lineages.

There must be, thus, much greater evolutionary complexity among humans than we usually assume. We can be happy, we should be happy, with the idea that, on the basis of ethnicities, some groups of peoples deserve special places in societies. We have to be careful, however. These special places do not have hard boundaries around them. They blend almost imperceptibly into one another. It is easy for us to enter a social or cultural trap. We should desire to preserve indigenous cultures, as we would want to preserve all cultures. But we must recognize that cultures do not have sharp biological boundaries. And, therefore, we must hope for everyone to have as good existences and advantages as everyone else. We must neither accept old hostilities that damaged old groups, nor make new hostilities against newly created, or newly migrated, groups.

As a result of all this, though genetic, cultural and sociological *races, tribes, ethnicities, etc.* are often thought of as separate, there are, in fact, enormous genetic, cultural and social continuities among humans. This is not to say that statistical peaks representing the centers (or means) of what may seem to be separate groups, are not distinguishable; they clearly are. But it is rather to say that, though there are recognizable visible peaks in the ethnic landscape, the peaks are low, melding almost indistinguishably(!) into one another; and that the valleys between them, in reality, are quite shallow, mixed, and very frequently crossed.

Thus, Figure 5.1 is an attempt to picture, what are generally thought of as separate races or ethnicities or tribes, as linked con-

Many peaks distinguishable, peaks meld closely

Edges of peaks not clearly classifiable.

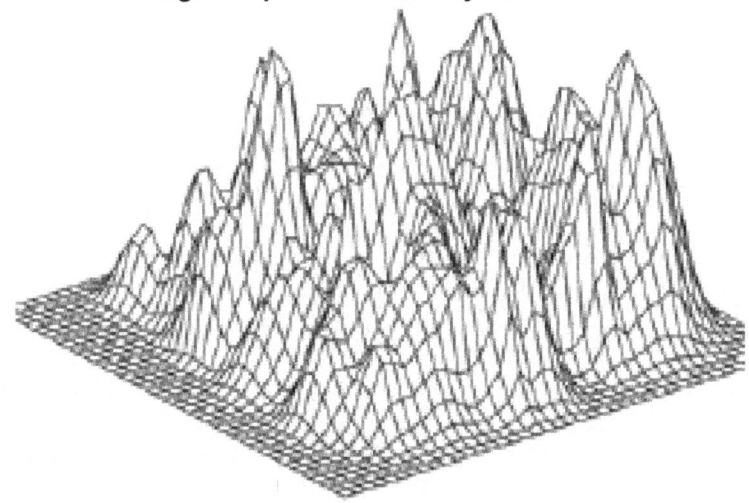

Fig. 5.1. Visualizing a pan-species — visible peaks but no clear margins, except at the absolute pan-species edge. And this is only a three-dimensional model of what, I am sure, is truly a multi-dimensional set of relationships.

tinuities evidenced only as visible peaks in a continuous species landscape. Humans, with a single landscape but many internal valleys and peaks, differ from many animals. Humans are thus a pan-species, (perhaps a relationships landscape paralleling Waddington's epigenetic landscape), with no clear separations overall. Peaks do exist and can be seen, and in that sense ethnicities have a reality. And it is not unreasonable that there would be recognition of and loyalty to such peaks. But it also makes sense that there should be recognition and loyalty across valleys (which, after all, are not very deep). And, therefore, there should also be recognition and loyalty to the entire landscape, to entire humanity.

I believe this picture, a crude model perhaps at this stage, is a reasonably correct description of the real links of humans today. Would that we could act it out, in our relationships within ourselves, with one another, even among us all, all humans? Such molecular information as we now have, suggests that these links have been true of humans not only for thousands of years, but for tens of thousands, even perhaps, for hundreds of thousands of years.

Yet opposite, separatist, views hold great sway in many humans, within many societies, especially among many nationalities today!

Thus, although we often self-identify as separate groups with different skin colors, with special languages, with particular social and cultural features, with recognitions of family links (often spurious, and, often, conversely, not recognized), with individual agonistic activities, with specific group aggressions, with separate religions, and separate land attachments, we are not independently separate. The extent of such separations as we perceive are internally generated.

We (humans) are a 'pan-species'.

To summarize: when it comes to assessing earlier forms, the fossil hunters and storytellers still tend to see almost every new find as especially important! The number of fossils that, when first found, are immediately designated 'critical', or the 'earliest', or the 'most important', or 'pre-human', or 'early human', or even just 'human' is too large. The number that are said to show evidence of human functions such as bipedality, or tool use, or specific social activity, is also unusually large. In contrast, the number that might be ancestors of apes is still incredibly small (one fossil pre-chimpanzee, and that just a few teeth). And the number that might, that just might, be ancestral to neither apes nor humans, seems to be almost zero!

Assessing Relationships

The standard ways of trying to assess the fossils, finding out which fossils are related to which, and eventually to which living species they are related, include, nowadays, character analyses. Characters are defined, counted, even measured, and the numbers used to estimate degrees of similarity through presence or absence in different forms.

However, it turns out that biological characters are not just a matter of measuring or counting, they also contain biological information about mechanisms and processes. I was first led in this analytical direction by almost accidental findings from the relationships between the dissections of muscles and the measurements of bones that they move. The relationships between bone and muscle in extant species provide information about the biology of anatomies: how they function, how they work. Could analysis of bones in fossil species alone, with insights from bone–muscle functional interrelationships in living species give more insights into functional differences in evolution, and on occasion, therefore into the nature of evolutionary change?

I fell into these ideas as a result of almost accidental findings as a first-year medical student.

Studies of the distributions of characters (mostly anatomical, but also more recently other kinds of characters: genetic, molecular) are especially used to model evolutionary change. Yet such studies often look only at the numbers. They often fail to take account of the biology behind the numbers. For example, almost all characters change during development, as well as being different as a result of evolution.

I love a story relevant to this point brought to my attention by our curator of bodies. He, Daryl Kirk, was responsible for the preservation of bodies and the preparation of skeletons in our dissecting room. On one occasion the carcass of an adult orangutan was made available by the local zoo. Daryl macerated the specimen, cleaned and dried the bones, and articulated them in a natural position within an arboreal diorama — quite a big job.

However, at the end of this task he came to me with a problem. In his hand, he had two small bones. "Where do these go, Prof?" he asked, in puzzlement. He was like a watch repairer, wondering where to put two leftover cog wheels!

Of course, all of his experience was with human materials. He did not know that the great apes have an additional small bone, the *os centrale* in the center of the wrist. This seems like a character that separates all apes and all humans. Such a character, described numerically amongst the species, adds to the taxonomic separation indicated: apes versus humans.

However, the picture is actually more complicated. Even humans do sometimes have an *os centrale* because this ossification, normally fusing with another carpal in humans during early growth, sometimes remains separate. (Indeed, when found in a human child on radiography, it can be mistaken for a fracture.) In apes, it almost always remains separate (hence receiving its own special name, *os centrale*). Though it might be thought characteristic of a taxonomic difference between apes and humans, it is actually a marker of a variation in developmental process that can be found in most apes and in some humans (especially human cretins, a congenital thyroid deficiency condition with reduced growth patterns). This is not a character of a taxonomic difference, but a feature of different developmental timing.

There are a number of such features that are known. Let us first confine our attention to information from species today.

In species living today, we have the ability to check individual soft tissue characters, e.g. muscle groups, and even overall anatomical complexes such as limb segments. These are not usually available in fossils. The very first example that I found was in the masseter muscle block responsible for jaw closing (Figure 5.2).

This phenomenon is widespread in upper limbs, in comparisons of humans and their closest living relatives (but, interestingly,

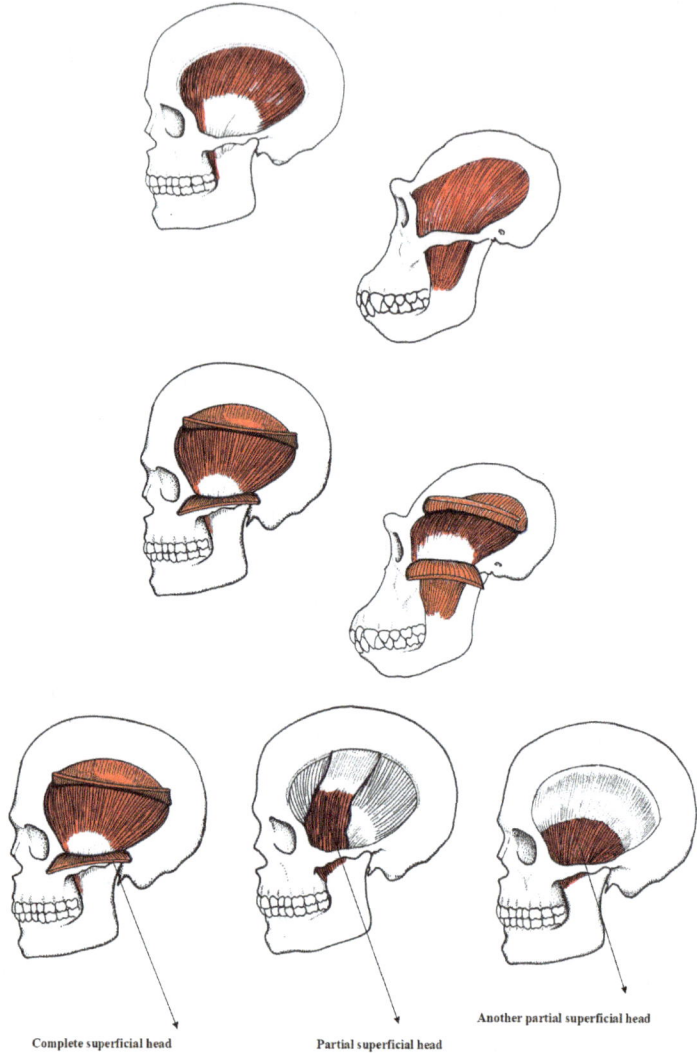

Fig. 5.2. The top row shows the differences normally observed between humans and chimpanzees in the external form of the jaw closing masseter muscle (red in the diagram) with apparently no tendon (white in the human diagram) whereas an entire fleshy external muscle is present in the chimpanzee. This is well known.

The middle row shows that dissection within the chimpanzee muscle finds that the tendon (white) is present — it is just that it is covered by this more superficial muscle sheet (red). This picture contrasts (also middle row) with the finding of the (apparently) *chimpanzee condition* in a human (a finding often called an anomaly).

The bottom row shows three different examples of such *anomalies* occasionally found in humans in any dissecting room.

not in lower limbs). This may relate to differences in the mechanics of mastication in humans versus apes.

Two, of many similar examples for upper limb muscle blocks are also known (Figure 5.3). Again, the extra complexities may relate to different mechanical usages of limbs (large mechanical forces in locomotion in all four limbs in non-human primates in comparison to reduced upper limb forces in non-locomotor upper limbs of fully bipedal humans).

These are not just two small simple differences, but quantitative variations (the extra muscle heads are usually small and weak). And there are not just a few, but many such variations in the musculature of the upper limbs in primates.

Interestingly and importantly, variations of this type are not found in lower limb muscle blocks!

We can move from soft tissues (like muscles) to fleshy limb parts (like digits). Again, there are some interesting differences, for example, in the hands and feet of primates (Figure 5.4).

Both hands and feet take up the mechanical loads of locomotion in the apes; the foot alone is involved in locomotion, and so the hand is much weaker, in bipedal humans.

To what degree are such notions also expressed in information about bones, and therefore available for fossils?

One simple example is the structure of the sternum in apes and humans (something that can be readily verified in museum specimens, Figure 5.5).

This is not an unusual type of finding. It can also be seen in the kneecap (Figure 5.6). A particular fossil showed two facets on the kneecap (top left). The modern human does not have these facets (top right). But the three figures below show that, on occasion, such facets are apparent in modern humans. Once again, they are not *yes–no* characters; they are quantitatively time

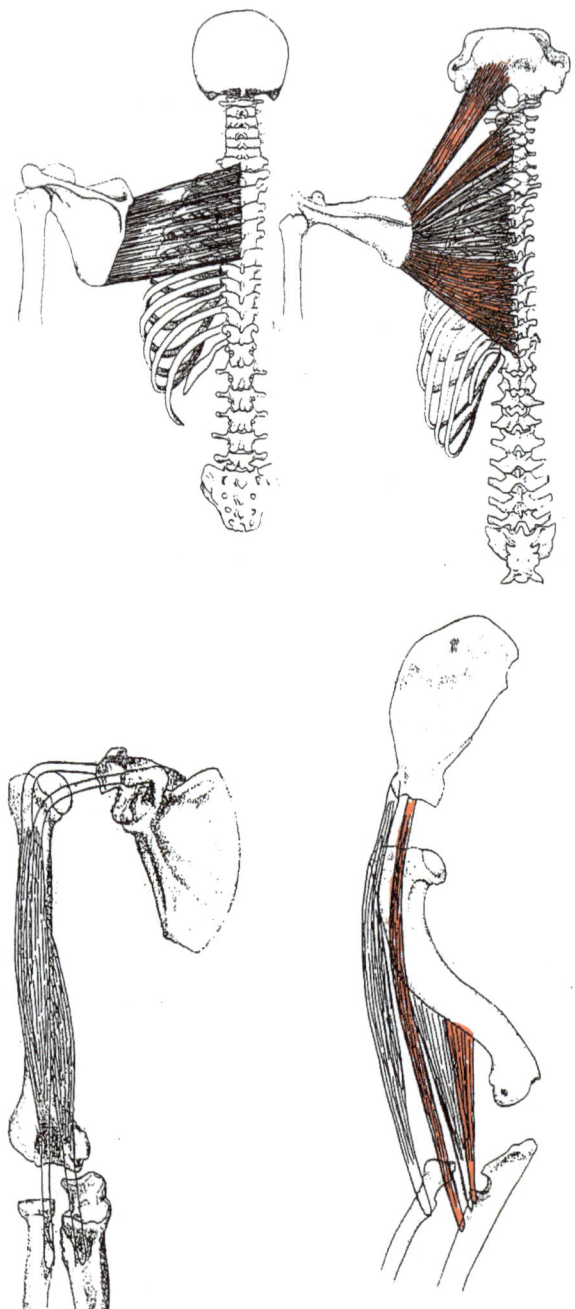

Fig. 5.3. Differences between simple muscle heads in humans, left diagrams, and complex muscles in non-human primates, right diagrams. But the extra heads (red) in non-human primates can all be found in individual humans.

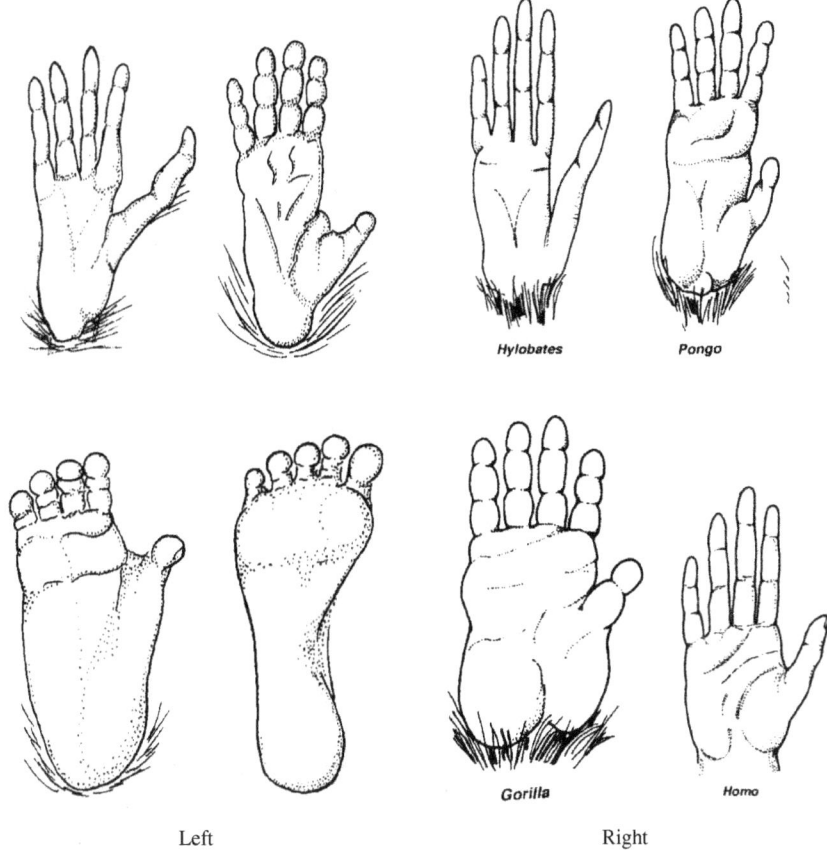

Fig. 5.4. Feet (left) and hands (right), at same foot size and in due hand proportion, in three apes and a human.

dependent. Again, such a characterization in a fossil might lead to a wrong determination.

I choose pictures of bones because, of course, it is bones that are most evident in the fossil record. And among bones, it is complexity of skulls that are so frequently studied for such evidence of relationships. Thus, instead of simply using a few characters of a skull, modern methods apply many landmarks to characterize complex features (Figures 5.7 and 5.8).

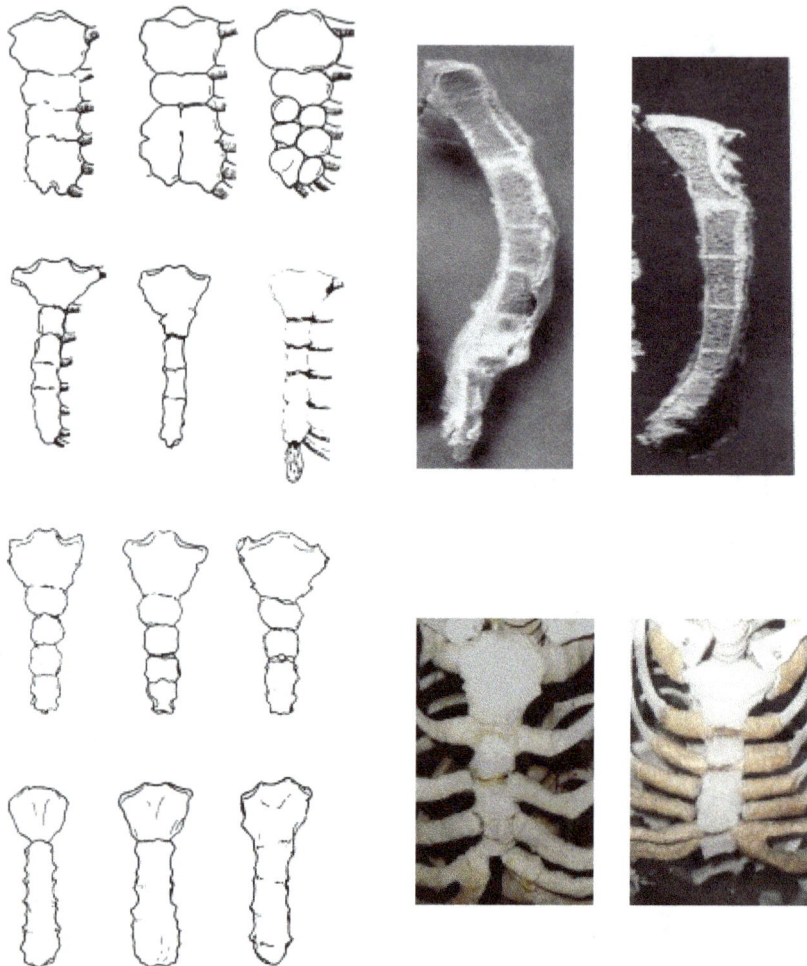

Fig. 5.5. Left columns: drawings of the complete segmentation of the sternum in three adult great apes (gorilla, chimpanzee and orangutan, upper three drawings) compared with those of three normal adult humans (essentially unsegmented — lowest diagram).

Right columns: photographs of sections of particular human sternums (above), and of articulated human sternums (below), showing that the lack of segmentation, which normally fuses much earlier in most humans, is sometimes delayed. As a result, in these cases individual humans look as though they have the sternal characters of apes. In other words, these features of the sternum are not individual characters diagnostic of taxonomy, but of developmental and epigenetic variations in growth and maturity. Fusion of the sternal segments occurs much earlier in humans than in apes. This feature, not understood, could result in a wrong characterization of a fossil.

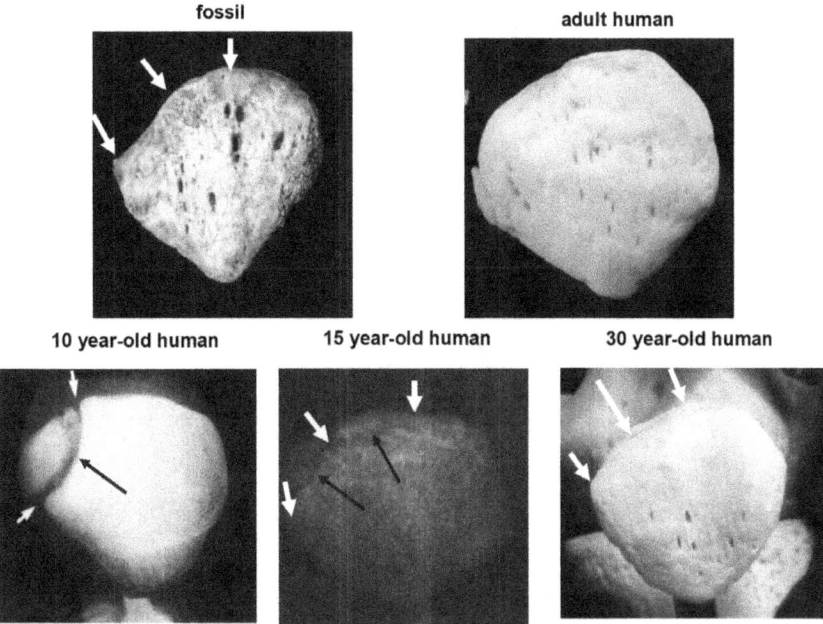

Fig. 5.6. Variations in human kneecaps compared to a pre-human fossil kneecap.

Such choice of landmarks can define different aspects of underlying bone biology (Figure 5.9). The positions of some of these landmarks are shown in diagrammatic sections (Figure 5.10).

The data arising from measurements of these landmarks provides the following transformation diagrams (Figure 5.11).

The new landmarks visualize the differences produced by recognizing the points resulting from the shell carved out by bone joints, and shell of muscle markings. The upper plot shows the result of not recognizing these differences, the lower, of accounting for them. This complexity recalls Thom's work on catastrophe theory (Figure 5.12).

The following frames (Figure 5.13) represent the development of a series of possible anatomical 'waves', *foldings*, (umbi-

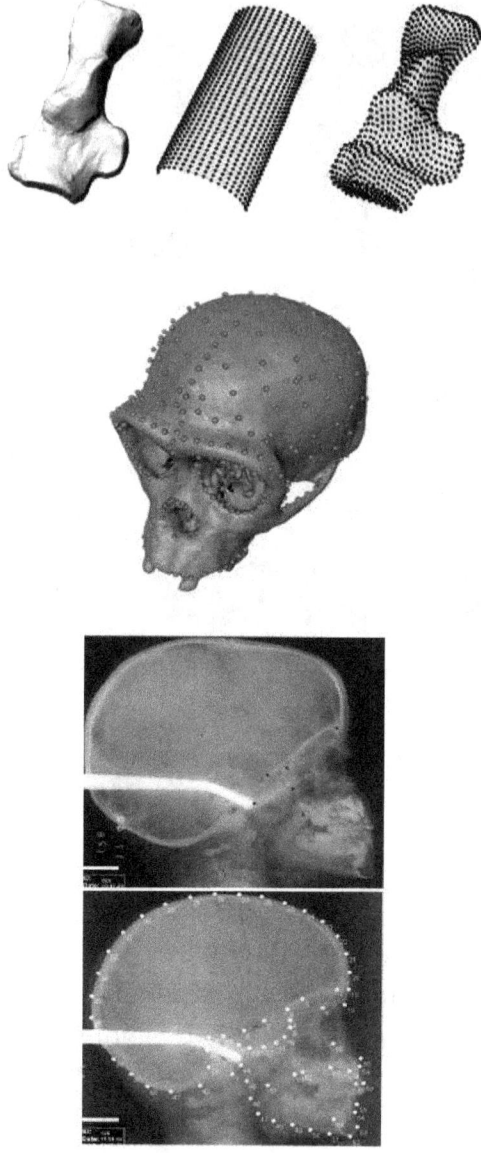

Fig. 5.7. A bone can (metaphorically speaking) be overlaid by a net giving rise to many landmarks from which measurements can be taken (computationally).

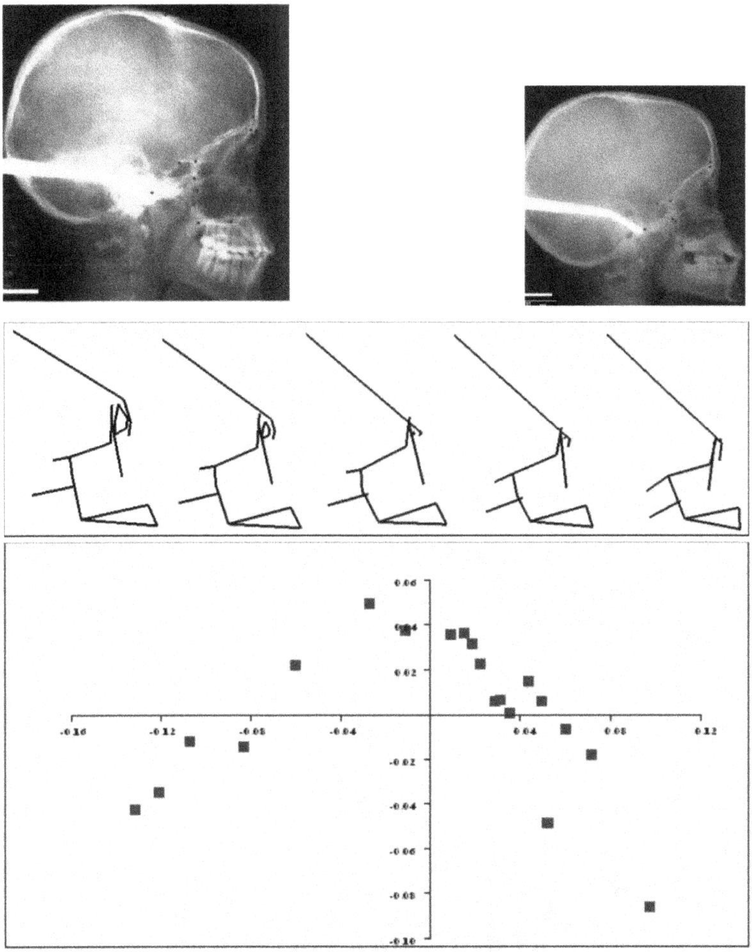

Fig. 5.8. How the landmarks of Fig. 5.7 give rise to plots of change with growth.

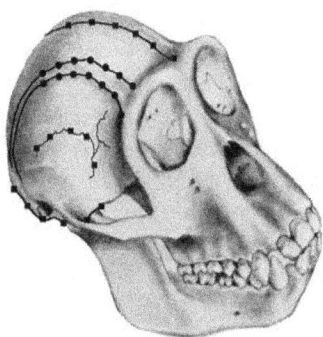

Fig. 5.9. Careful choice of landmarks define different aspects of the underlying biology of a bone. Small circles are landmarks of muscle attachments, small squares, of joint contacts.

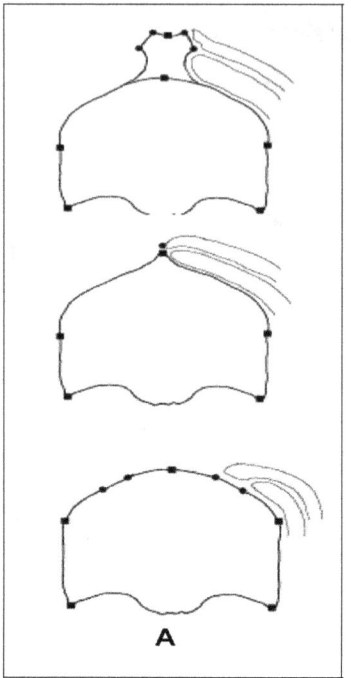

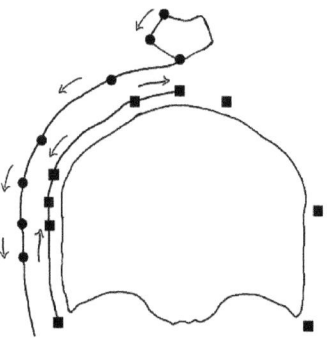

Fig. 5.10. Showing how some measurements are displayed in relation to different external features. Upper frames show bony features resulting from muscle attachments and joint surfaces. The first frame shows a large sagittal crest with two ridges, the second shows where the two lines come together forming a single sagittal line but with no lips. The third shows where the two temporal lines never come together.

The fourth diagram shows the two sets of points 'move' in different directions in the comparisons.

(Again, small circles are of muscle attachments, small squares of joint contacts).

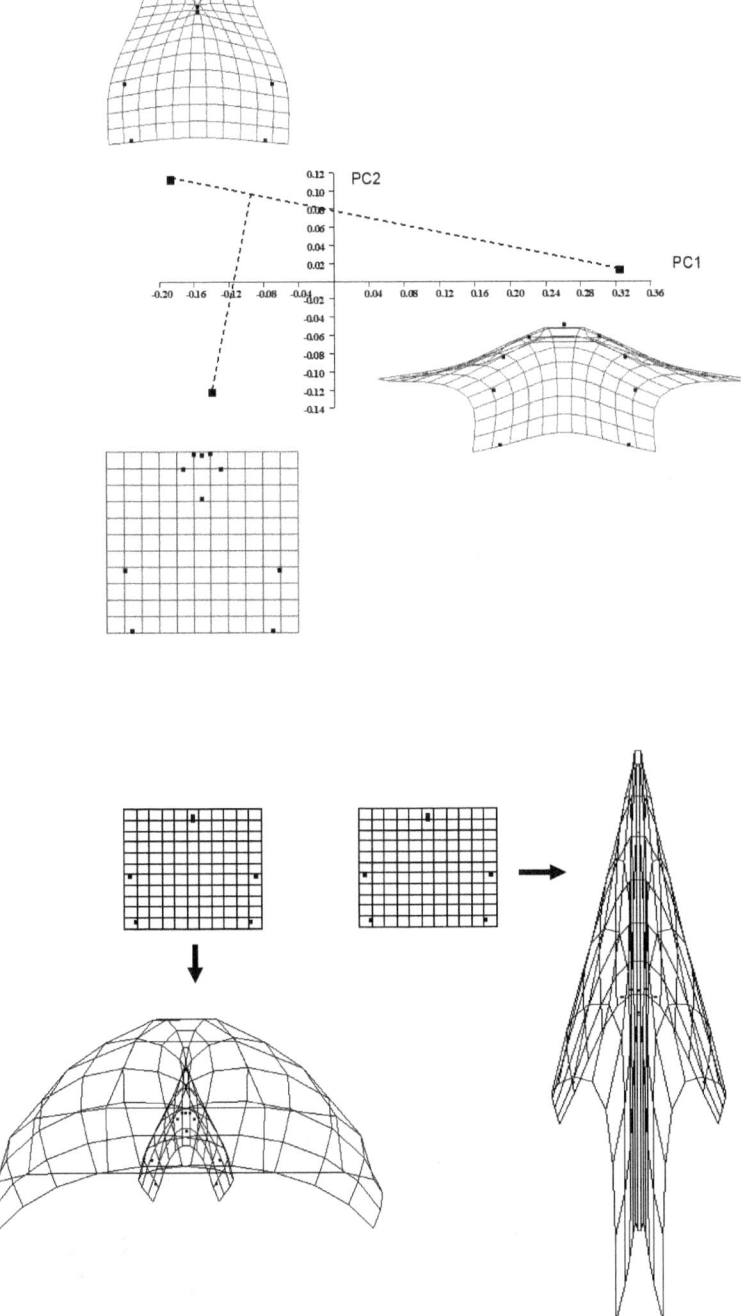

Fig. 5.11. Examples of analyses of one each of these three skulls: above, using standard geometric landmarks, and below, using the new functional landmarks.

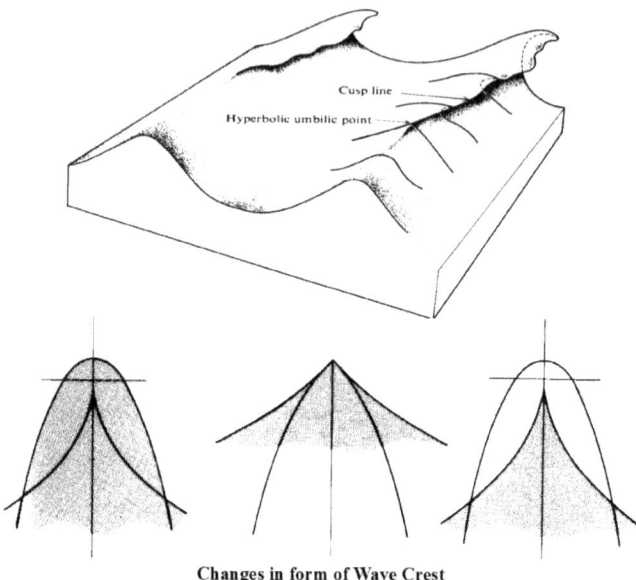

Changes in form of Wave Crest

Fig. 5.12. Upper frame: the changes in and along a crest figured as a diagram of a 'real' wave breaking. Lower figures: the changes at particular points along the wave crest.

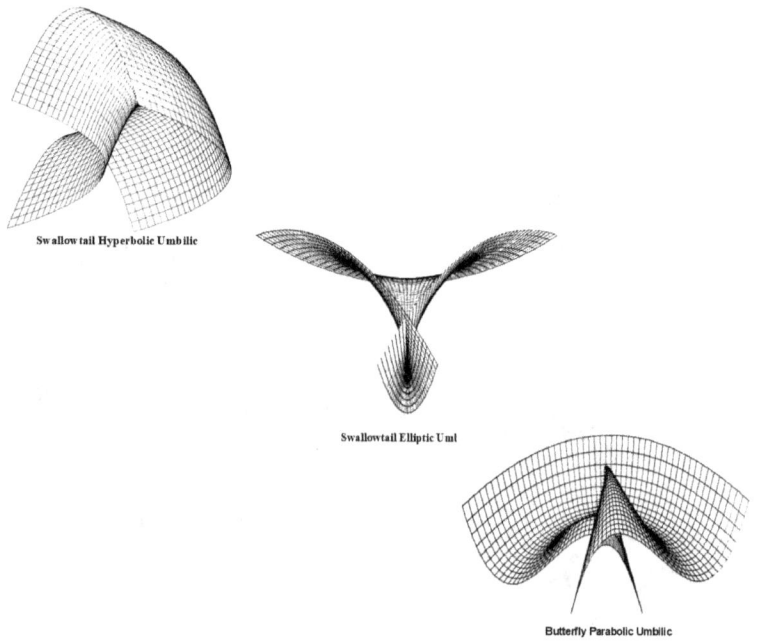

Fig. 5.13. A variety of foldings.

lici), occurring as a result of changes during development or evolution. It is fascinating, as before, that such ideas also exist in art (Chapter 1). They allow us to visualize, even better understand, differences or changes that are complex.

Do mathematical figures like these have any potential, possibly just descriptive, possibly biologically explanatory, in dealing with novelty, loss, and discontinuities, in structure, in function, in development and growth, and therefore, also in evolution? These ideas suggest that something new is needed. Can we join such ideas for both fossils and living species (Figure 5.14 and its table)?

Modelling these Ideas

The day came when I thought it might actually be possible to model these ideas computationally. However, at that point, my computer skills were not good enough. So, I decided to simulate possibilities by tossing dice to make 'evolutionary' decisions.

This has been done before in science (even if Einstein famously said "God does not play dice").

Of course, my game was very simple. I tried to imitate the effects, on simple genealogies of individuals; of 'breedings' and of 'migrations'. At first, I did it with male/female pairs and their offspring (Figure 5.15).

In this model, the particular descendants that migrated to the third region, one fairly soon after the first migration, and two backwards migrations later (if you can go one way, you may be able to go the other!) occurred using the dice. Then, I converted this picture to show only the links from the first migration (Figure 5.16).

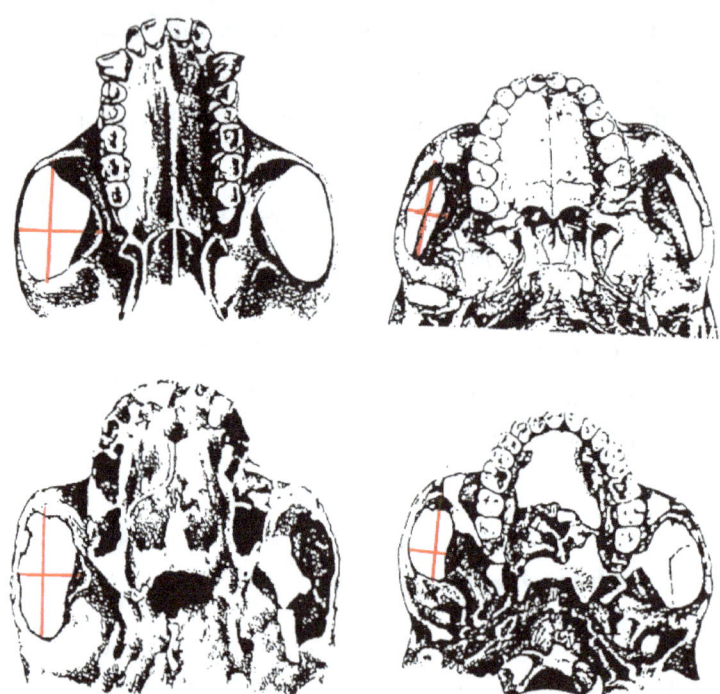

Extant species	Fossils pecies
GREAT APES 0.74–0.88 Heavy temporal muscle including large superficial head	**AUSTRALOPITHECUS 0.73-0.80** Do we assume heavy temporal muscle including large superficial head?
MODERN HUMANS 0.60 Light temporal muscle with superficial head absent	**ANCIENT HUMANS 0.63** Presumably we assume same?
	FLORES FOSSIL 0.73 (est.) What do we assume?

Fig. 5.14. and Table. How the size of the temporalis (jaw) muscle might influence the size and shape of the bony zygomatic arch of the skull. It can be measured as a simple index, in red, in an extant ape and human (above), and two fossils (australopithecine and early human, below). That index can be tabulated as in the table, with a possible implication indicated!

Dangerous Differences: Race and Ethnicity, Kindred and Ancestors 101

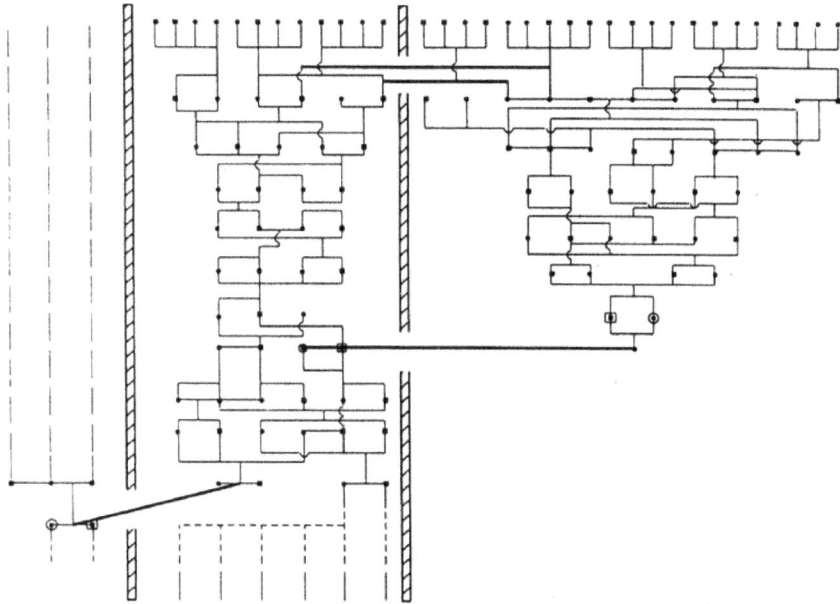

Fig. 5.15. A simple genealogy of individuals starting from a male/female pair in one (geographic) region (bottom left in the diagram), migrating across a barrier (the left hatched vertical line) to a second region already containing individuals, and then producing its own descendants together with further migrations across another barrier (the right hatched vertical line).

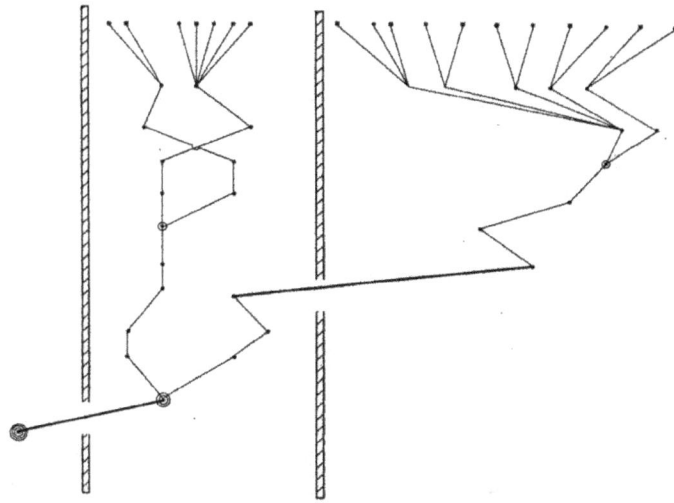

Fig. 5.16. The effect of this suggests there is a complete separation between the groups across the barriers (producing, apparently, a new separate group).

But further migrations also stemmed from individuals already in the second migration. These gave rise to more migrations into the third region. Thus, the picture became more complex, especially more mixed (Figure 5.17).

As a result of this I became bolder. I attempted further models. Thus, Figure 5.18 shows four populations of individual lineages and their interconnections in one run.

Further attempts show differences between four different runs of Fig. 5.18 (Figure 5.19).

These four different runs show the various interconnections, including migrations, between the four evolving populations. There are some marked differences between the runs.

Of course, the differences across this small armchair example (and I did many of them) merely egged me on. So, I tried slightly more complex modelling, this time, of simulated species, rather than

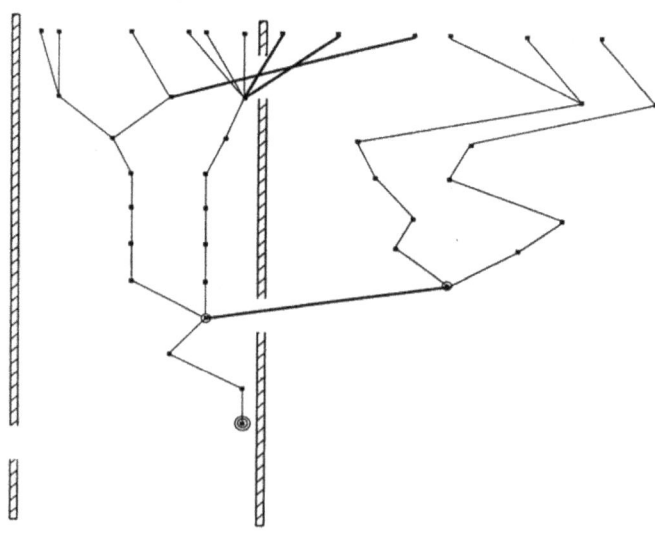

Fig. 5.17. Further migrations occurred. The populations in the second and third migrations are complexly related.

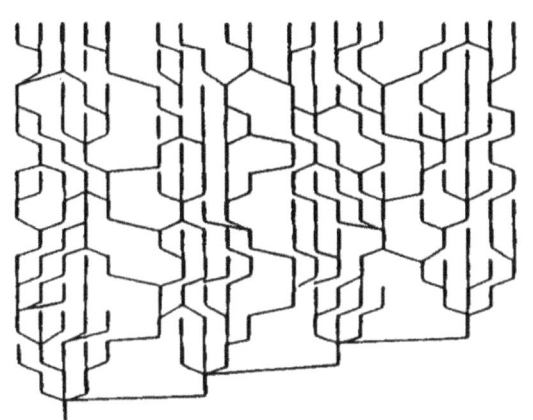

Fig. 5.18. Above, four populations of lineages, and below, their interconnections.

simulated individuals, but it needed a computer program, devised by Ken Wessen, who had come to work with me (Figure 5.20).

In other words, drawing inferences from the **characters of fossil specimens alone** almost always leads to totally false relationships. For example, the lower left-hand analysis (the paleontologist's analysis) of Figure 5.20 implies that all the living forms arose from a single, recent fossil. The lower right-hand analysis

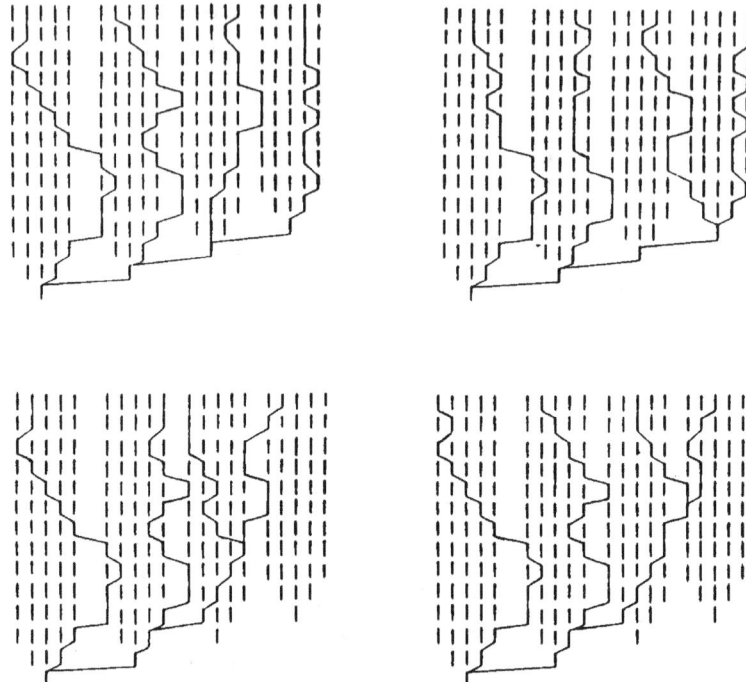

Fig. 5.19. Four different runs of the model interconnections of Fig. 5.18.

(the real picture) shows that the extant species actually evolved from an ancestral species very much further back in time.

This thinking might have gone no further (though the idea has been published), if it had not been for Dr. Wessen's further work. Ken Wessen, already with a PhD in theoretical plasma physics, came wanting to do a Masters with me, applying his computational skills in mathematical modelling to evolutionary biology. As soon as I found out how deep his ideas were, I persuaded him to change to a second PhD. That second doctoral thesis was the shortest I have ever supervised (213 pages, but awarded Top Honors, and published in whole by Cambridge University Press). He first set up a better genealogy system. Figure 5.21 shows two short simple examples: the determination of the mother of us all,

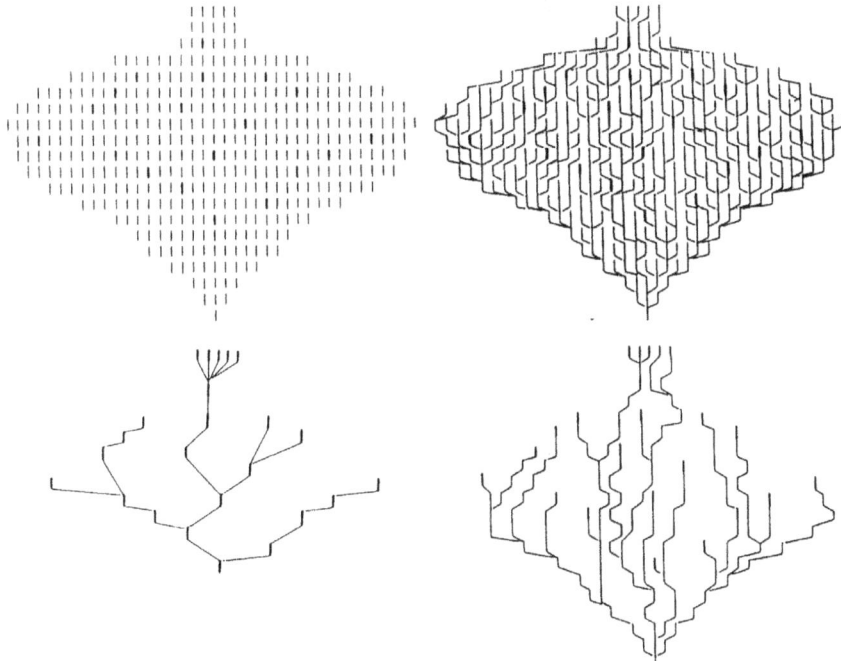

Fig. 5.20. A computer-simulated genealogy of species (the small vertical lines), starting with an initial species at the base, and evolving upwards into an ampulla-shaped pattern of species.

The upper left frame shows all species without connections, both found species (fossils, bold vertical lines), and not-found species (light vertical lines). The upper right-hand frame shows the complicated total picture. The lower left-hand frame shows the paleontologist's view as determined from characters of found-fossil species (bold) alone. The lower right-hand frame shows the true relationships of the living species to all the older species. The relationships of the entire graph, the true picture, is completely different from that obtained from the characters of the fossils alone (lower left-hand frame).

and the father of us all, from a base of individuals ten generations back!

This was further elaborated in the following model (Figure 5.22) which gives one example of what must happen a great deal in evolution. It simulates the effects, on a group of evolving species, of climactic, geologic, astronomic, or ecological catastrophes producing a bottleneck (when the whole thing nearly goes extinct).

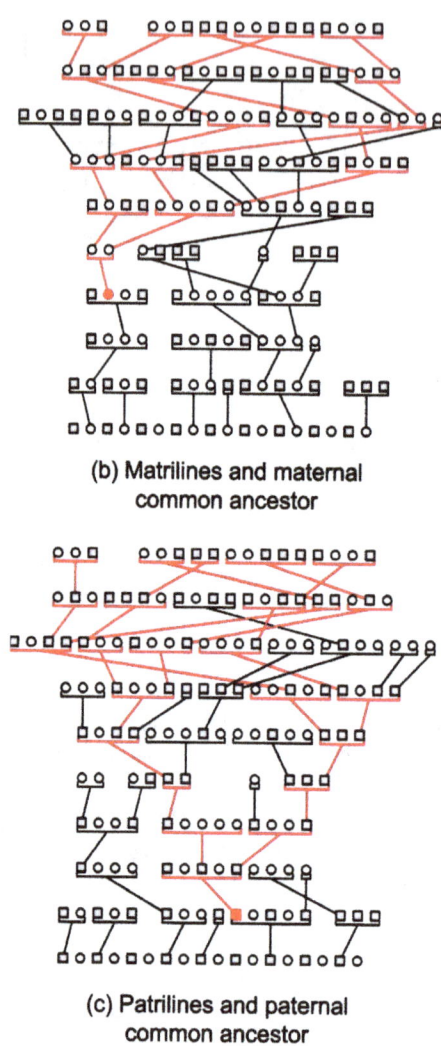

Fig. 5.21. Upper frame: the mother of us all is in the 6th generation back. The lower frame shows that the father of us all is in 9th generation, 50 percent further back.

The relationships of the characters of the known fossils in this model imply that the common ancestor of all the living species is just five species generations from the top (present). However, the reality is that the common ancestor is much earlier in time, at thirteen species generations back, only six species generations

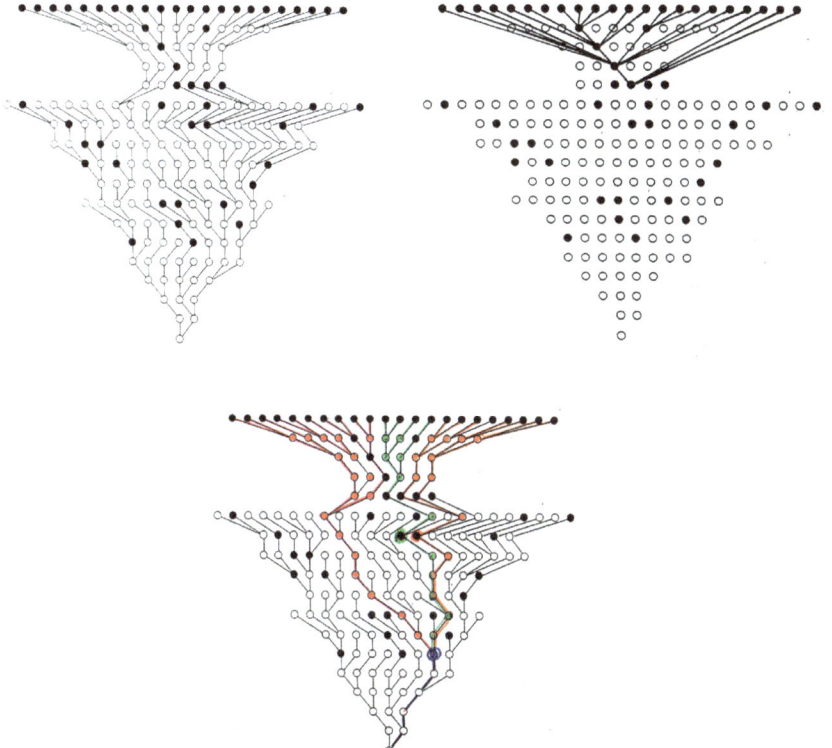

Fig. 5.22. A model of species evolving from the base to the top. There is a 'near extinction' event, bottleneck, near the top. Upper left frame: shows all species and all connections (solid dots show fossil species, open dots show species not found as fossils). Upper right frame shows the tree that can be calculated by analysis from the fossil characters alone, and it leads to all present-day species. The lower frame shows the 'real connections' and the 'real common ancestor' which is much further back in time. (Circled species of each color show first ancestors for each lineage.)

from the start. It also shows that, unlike assessment from the fossil characters alone, there are three separate lineages from that early common ancestor, not one. Character analysis of the fossil data alone is unable to find any of this complexity. Statistics derived from many such runs confirm this finding. It is, thus, necessary to be very skeptical of assessments based on the usual character analyses.

Another model (also from Ken Wessen's program) elaborated a *species-divergence system* that allowed for changes in: numbers of species generations, of characters for each species, of states for each character, of change of rate of characters, of selective advantages of characters, and of the possibility of splitting and merging (i.e. simulating both species separations and hybrid combinations). This model (Figure 5.23) shows that analyses

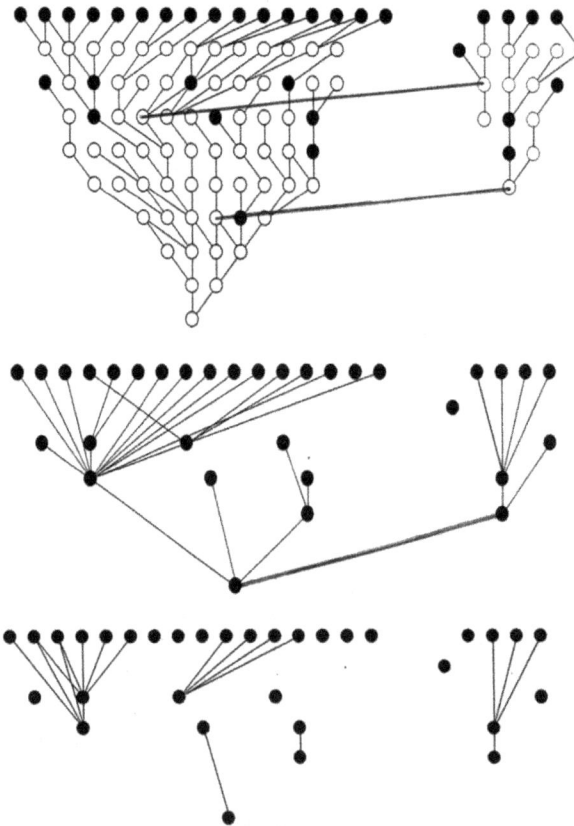

Fig. 5.23. The upper frame shows the real (modelled) effects of migrations with the true migrations being indicated as bold lines. The middle frame shows the single migration (bold), but a different one, that seems evident through looking only at characters for the found fossils. An incorrect migration is indicated! The lowest frame shows that no found fossils are involved in the migrations at all.

of the characters of fossils alone may not only give us **a wrong common ancestor**, but may not even allow **correct identification of migrations**.

And the matter of common ancestors is also complex (Figure 5.24).

The implications of doing many such runs are shown in Table 5.1. The true common ancestors are always much further back in time than common ancestors calculated from fossils alone.

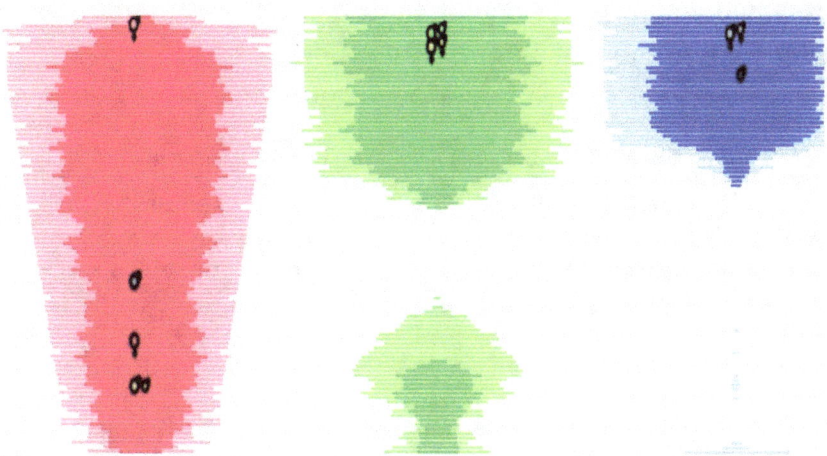

Fig. 5.24. 100 generations with two further migrated populations showing where the mothers and fathers of us all (the small sex icons) are, and showing also failed migrations (extinctions). Populating the continents must have been very complex!

Table 5.1. One example of the differences between apparent and true fossil links.

No of runs	Generations back to true common ancestor	Generations back to apparent common ancestor
52	18 (range 15–23)	8 (range 3–11)
28	0	10 (range 6–16)
20	0	0

Of course, one has to make many runs of models like these to get the statistics (Table 5.2). For example, the true numbers (averages) of fossil species lying on lineages leading to modern forms are many less than the apparent numbers. And the 'real' common ancestor of all the living species is far older (much further down), than the 'assumed' (wrongly) common ancestor.

Such analyses must be carried out many times to get statistics.

The numerical part of the output provides all the data, but the details of the relationships are not seen in the figure. However, the species lineages have completely different evolutionary pathways and completely different earliest ancestors in their various migrations (Figure 5.25).

Table 5.2. Number of fossils lying on extinct lineages.

No of runs	True average number of fossils lying on lineages leading to present-day species	Apparent average number of fossils reconstructed as lying on lineages leading to present-day species
1,000	14 out of 34	22 out of 34

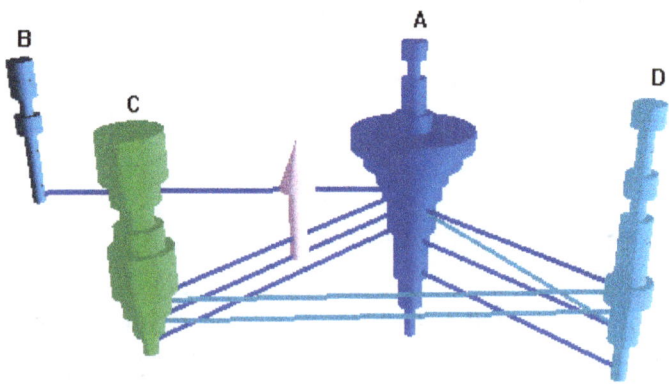

Fig. 5.25. An example of migrations among four 'continents' and over many species generations (details hidden by the many generations, but present in the numerical output).

This all implies that most fossils are unlikely to be on lineages leading to today's species! Yet paleoanthropologists usually place most fossils on lineages leading to the present day!

Developmental and Molecular Bases of Characters

Although earlier investigations were mostly worked out by simply comparing the anatomical characters of living species and fossils (the latter usually incomplete), today further information arises from knowledge of molecular changes. Again, however, these extra elements are, for fossils, usually very meagre and incomplete. As a result, if we use character analyses, we need to apply them with much circumspection.

For example, there can be major differences between the anatomical views and molecular views of species evolution. Figure 5.26 gives a simple example of this, showing that the tree of

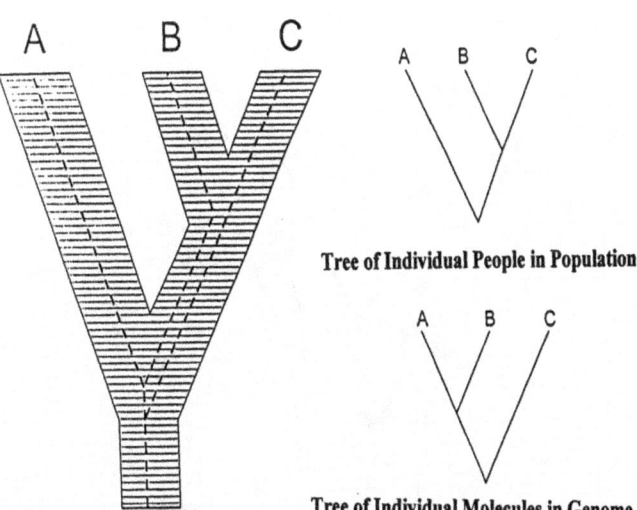

Fig. 5.26. A simple view of the difference between splits of samples of people in a population and splits in samples of molecules (genes) in the genome.

individual people in populations can be very different from the tree of individual molecules in genomes.

And the matter is really much more complex than that. Figure 5.27 shows how molecules may give even more different

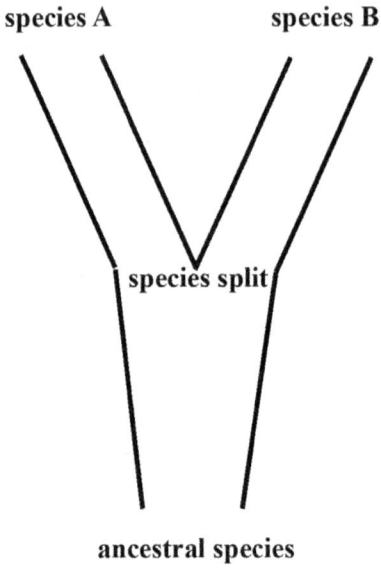

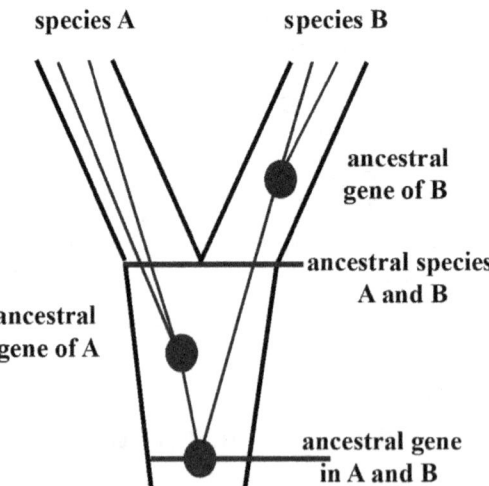

Fig. 5.27. Upper frame: splitting of species based on ancestral anatomical characters. Lower frame: different splittings based on ancestral genes.

answers than anatomies. A split of an ancestral species (based on anatomical characters) may appear to be at one evolutionary time (upper frame). But splits of ancestral genes will of course vary from gene to gene (lower frame).

It is now evident, of course, that there is a more complex relationship between anatomical characters and molecular precursors. This is shown for the muscles of mastication, Figure 5.28.

Finally, we can ask the question: can we expect to find evidence relating to muscles from studies of characters of bones (Figure 5.29)?

It is evident then, that character analysis without understanding of the underlying biology can provide misleading ideas.

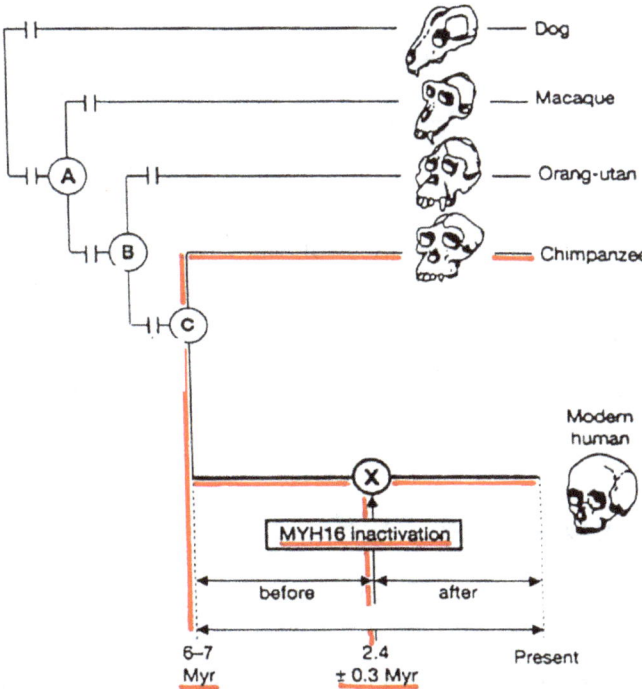

Fig. 5.28. The tree of the possible time of molecular MYH16 factor changes (inactivation) in humans.

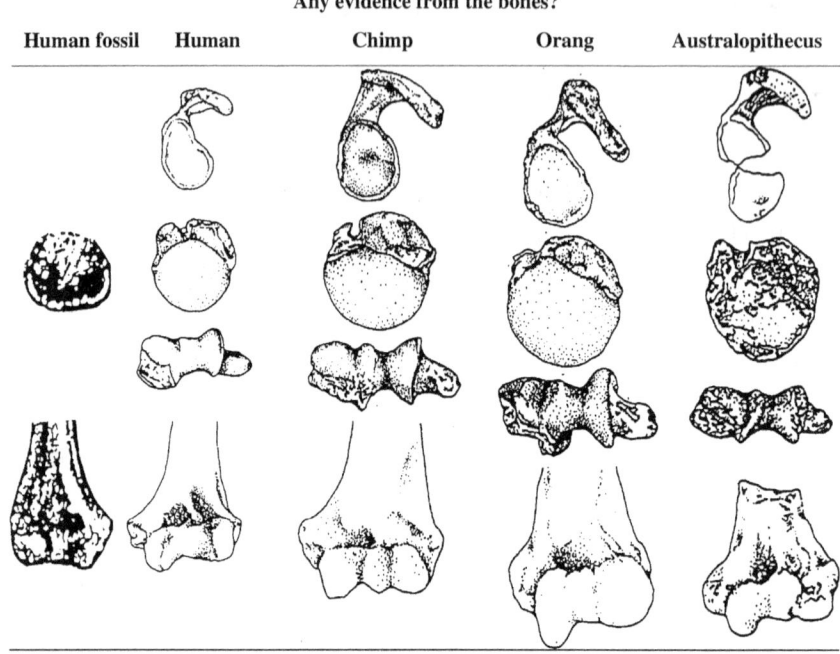

Fig. 5.29. Dimensions, correctly scaled, for articular surfaces of scapula and humerus, showing, that, like the muscles and the limbs of the upper limbs (above), the bones show the same relative size differences between humans and modern apes, and provide implications for fossils.

One of the further developments that stem from modelling evolutionary ideas resulted in a completely different set of findings. These came from my interests in China (see later). I attempted to understand the effects of modelling one-child policies.

Modelling One-Child Policies

Our first attempts at modelling one-child policies are shown in Figure 5.30.

Of course, though it seemed not to have occurred to the then Chinese government that this would be a natural effect of such a

Fig. 5.30. Models of one-child policies. Seventy-five (of one hundred) runs went extinct very early, example left frame (which is what one would expect)! Fifteen runs (example middle frame) lasted for a long time. But only five runs (example right frame) actually made it to the present day! (Apologies for the Moiré fringe artefacts in the diagram.)

policy over the long term, it is interesting to see that the modeling forecast the situation correctly.

These various studies mean that I have long been unhappy with the standard way of handling anatomical characters. Such molecular information as we have, both from fossils and living humans, indicates that the situation is far more complex.

Chapter 6
Aging and Death: Life Span, Mortality, Wellness and Illness!

Other important elements of human change are development, growth, wellbeing, aging, and death. These are especially important to anatomists! For me, they were exemplified by a birthday card (Figure 6.1) that I received from my wife recently.

So, You Want to Live Forever?

This led, of course, to thinking about just how long one might live. What prognostic measures of this do we have? Some are very obvious, such as **maximum life span**. This is not a good measure, being dependent on the age at death of one individual. A better measure is **average life span**, depending upon the average age at death of many people. But of course, this average includes many individuals who die early for reasons not related to aging. A third measure is **life expectancy**. This depends upon the length of life of a group of people born at the same period: an actuarial calculation for a cohort. Then there is **mortality**; this depends upon the proportion of actual deaths in a population (i.e. a figure based upon numbers of real deaths). Finally, there are the questions of **wellbeing** and **illness**, leading to **death**; how and why they change as we age.

The maximum life spans of some living things are quite surprising: e.g. Eternal God, Redwood, California, 12,000 years, and King's Holly, Tasmania, 43,000 years! Of course, I cheated by using

Fig. 6.1. The caption reads: It's All about the Thrill of the Chase!

the words *living things* for these plants. The maximum ages of animals seem much less, and include 188 years for a Malagasy Turtle, and 177 years for a Giant Tortoise. But, of course, these species are evolutionarily far distant from humans.

The best comparisons for humans might be thought to be other primates: apes and monkeys. One particular gorilla at the London Zoo achieved the age of 45.

But some surprising figures are provided by some surprising creatures, e.g. bird spiders at 30 years, leeches at 27, fruit flies at, say, 0.1 years, rotifers at 0.03 years, and some bacteria for only 20 minutes.

Other surprising figures are for the Sacred Lotus, recovered from a dry lake bed in NE China: 1,300 years, and the Judean Date Palm, Methuselah (Figure 6.2), at 2,000 years. And even these values are far exceeded by Siberian Flower seeds, dated at 31,800 years (by radiocarbon dating), yet with plants grown from those seeds from an ancient squirrel burrow!

Fig. 6.2. Methuselah.

Even these numbers are eclipsed by recent findings. Thus, some scientists have just revived bacteria which have survived more that 100 million years lying dormant on the sea floor, and are now reproducing. And goodness knows what might be brought back in dust from the bed of some long dried-out lake on the Moon or Mars?

Will such samples contain dormant spores of bacteria, or even dormant viroids of viruses, perhaps capable of being reawakened to reproduce?

And how old would they be; and, possibly, how dangerous?

Maximum Life Span of Humans(!)

Of course, at his death, Adam was 930 years old, Methuselah, 969. At the flood, Isaac was 180 and Jacob 147. In isolated mountainous places such as Georgia, the Andes and Shangri La some people were said to live to 150 plus. There are also some putative ages for the Middle Ages: Henry Jenkins died December 1670, said to be 169; Thomas Par died November 1635, said to be 152, and Catherine, Countess of Desmond, died in 1604, said to be at 140!

How are these figures obtained? Tongue in cheek: such figures for longevity are based on many factors: very hard agrarian work, gentle quiet restful lifestyle, moderate food intake, vegetarianism, meat eating, no wheat food, no alcohol, regular alcohol, red wine, scotch (for the Scots), abstinence from sex, regular sex, some other form of sex! *"And either deliberate cheating, or accidental miscounting!!"*

In contrast to the above figures, genuine historical estimates are said to give figures for expectation of life at birth of, say, 20–25 in the first century AD, 35–40 at the end of the 18th century in Europe and North America, 70+ by 1970 in North America, and 84 by 1990, for North American women. Individual figures of 110–114 were recorded for named individuals: Pierre Joubert, and seven others, all females. When I first looked into this matter, the oldest person (fully recorded, Figures 6.3 and 6.4) was a woman, aged 122 (France). When she died, the oldest woman was

Fig. 6.3. Jeanne Calment at 117: smoked for all her adult life!

Aging and Death: Life Span, Mortality, Wellness and Illness! 121

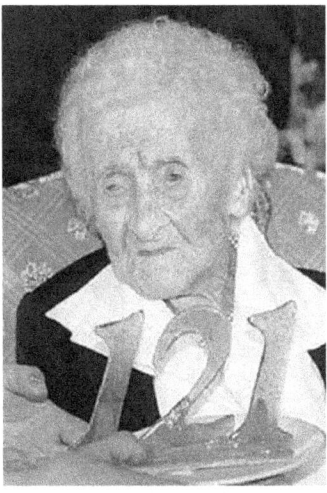

Fig. 6.4. Jeanne Calment died at 122!

Fig. 6.5. Misao Okawa at 117.

119 (Pennsylvania). And when she died, the oldest woman was 107 (Australia), see also Figures 6.5 to 6.7.

(But a Russian mathematician is casting doubt on the Calment record. Nikolay Zak, of the Moscow Centre for Continuous Mathematical Education, said in a report that he believes that Calment was actually Yvonne Calment, Jeanne's daughter, who had assumed her mother's identity to avoid inheritance taxes in the 1930s. That would have made her 99 when she died.

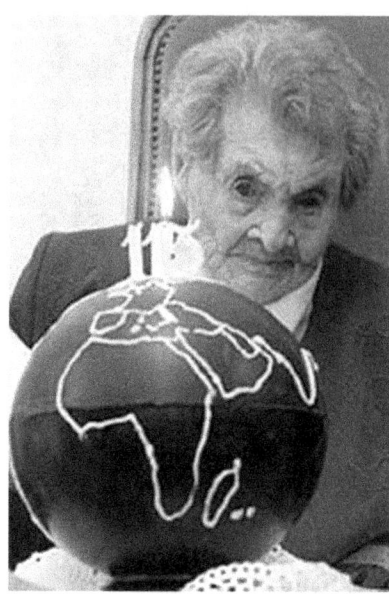

Fig. 6.6. Marie Bremont and Earth-shaped birthday cake at her 115th party.

Fig. 6.7. Jack Lockett (Australia) at his 110th birthday with his great grandson, aged nine.

The evidence produced by Zak in a paper published recently on ResearchGate is said not to be definitive. But it does sound likely; and it would not have been the first fiddling with birth records!

It is true there was someone said to be even older: Elizabeth Israel from the Dominican Republic claimed to be 125! But a birth certificate, required as proof, was said to be lost.

The normal female/male ratio for centenarians is about 5:1. However, in Sardinia the female/male centenarian ratio is 1:1. Special DNA factors (Figure 6.8) may be involved (found in twenty percent of these Sardinian male centenarians, but only two percent of Italian males).

Immunological factors are also important. Thus, immune responses (T and B lymphocytes) tend to diminish with age. Innate immunity (activity of macrophages) tends to improve with age.

External environment is likely also important. Thus, in Sardinia there is a healthy low stress agrarian lifestyle, and everyone drinks local red wine in abundance (elixir of life).

Age changes are shown in Figures 6.9 to 6.12.

There is a condition called progeria (Figure 6.13), once thought to be premature aging. In it, 15–18-year-old children appear as little old men and women. They usually die of cardiovascular effects, but most physiological and psychological function tests give results normal for their real chronological ages. *Progeria is probably nothing to do with aging but a rare disease with a superficial resemblance to aging.* And there are many different progerias!

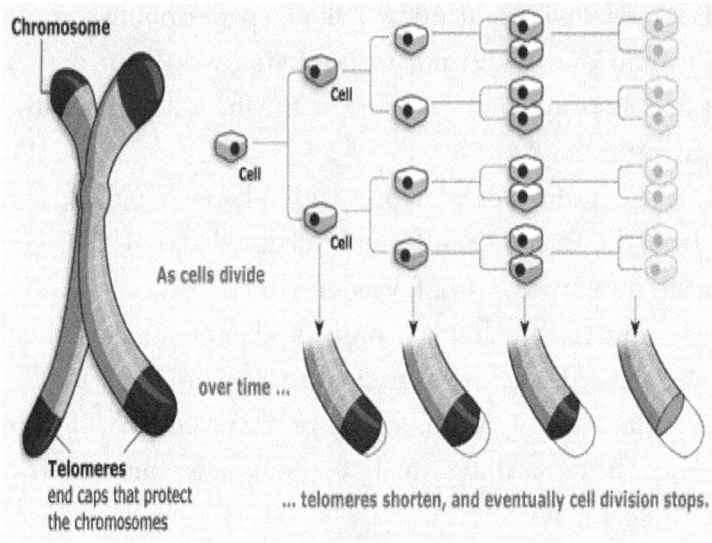

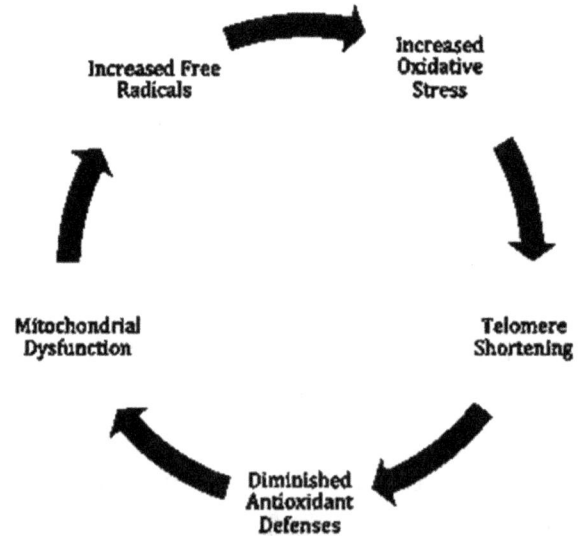

Fig. 6.8. Is part of the aging process a telomere shortening cycle?

Life Expectancy

Another measure is life expectancy (Figures 6.14 and 6.15). This is a statistical estimate of how long people may expect to live. This is

Aging and Death: Life Span, Mortality, Wellness and Illness! 125

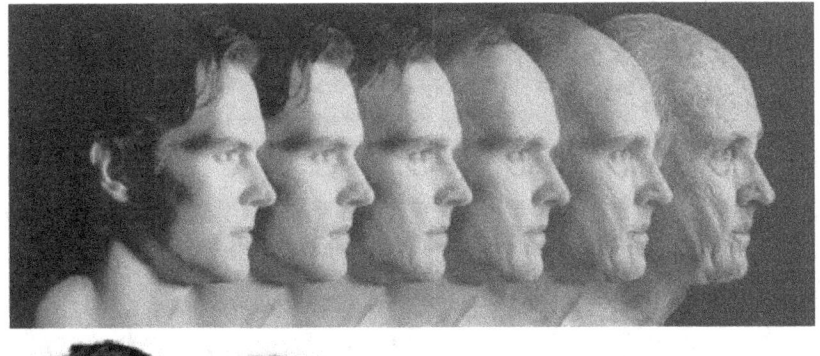

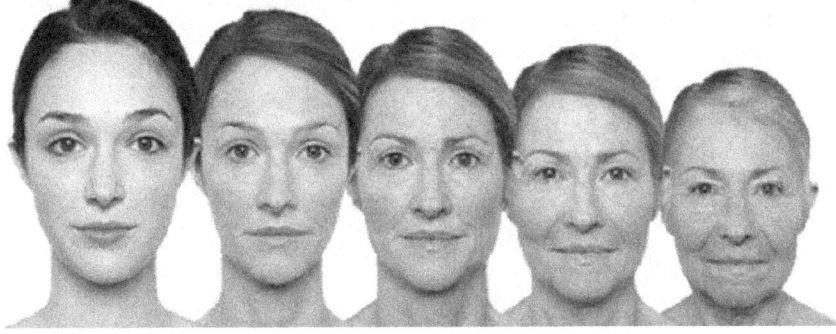

Fig. 6.9. Facial changes with aging: do you really want to know?

important to the insurance industry, and for anyone planning for the future.

Another source of life expectancy information, with costs, is shown in Figure 6.15.

But the critical data about life expectancy is its gender imbalance (Figures 6.16 and 6.17).

There are also differences in life expectancy in different countries, Figure 6.18.

There is also a difference in the costs of living a long life (Figures 6.19 and 6.20).

Several nations show serious recent changes in life expectancies (Figure 6.21).

Comparable information about life expectancy has been available for many nations since the 1960s (Figure 6.22).

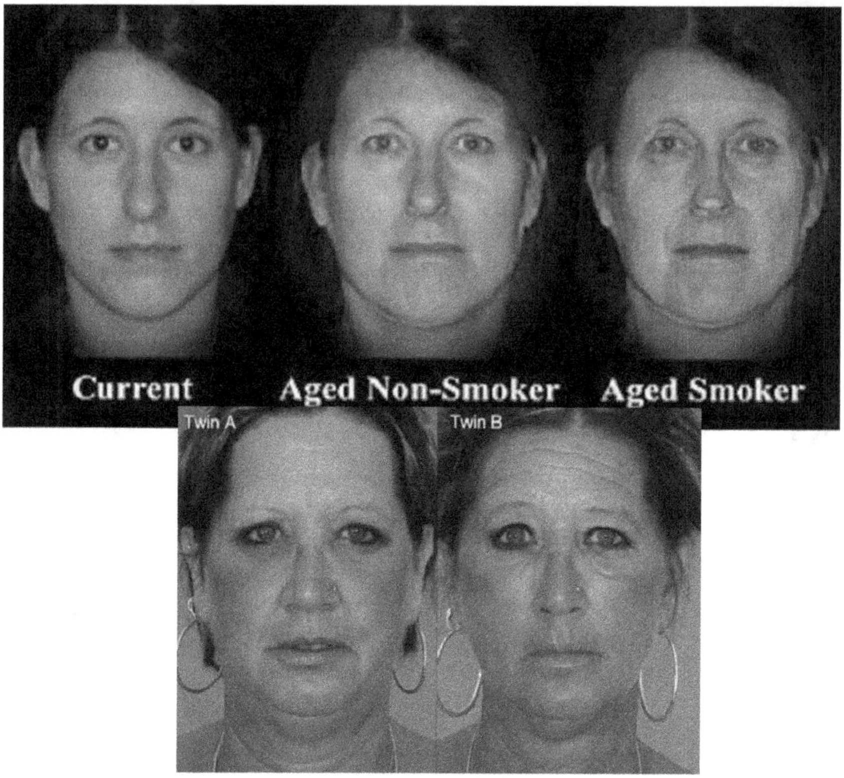

Fig. 6.10. Further facial changes: upper row designed to frighten you — but, of course, done with Photoshop. The lower row should frighten you: twins but only the right-hand one (with marked facial wrinkles) smoked!

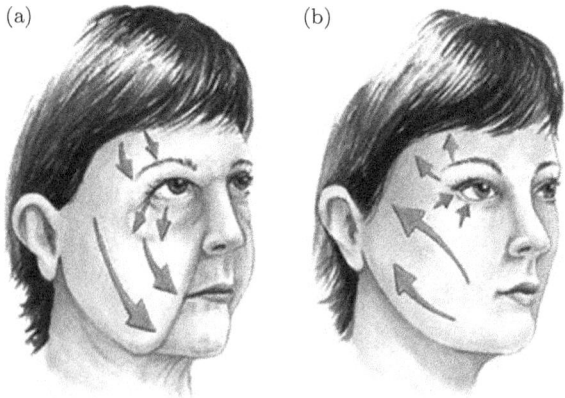

Fig. 6.11. Fixing the problem with surgery or Botox!

Fig. 6.12. And when baby did talk!

And equivalent data have been used to estimate what the changes might be in the future (Figures 6.23 to 6.25). The accuracy, or otherwise, of such future estimates are evident by looking at new data as they have come along.

On the basis of these real figures for 1987, Figure 6.23 shows the future estimates that were made in 1987 for ten years later.

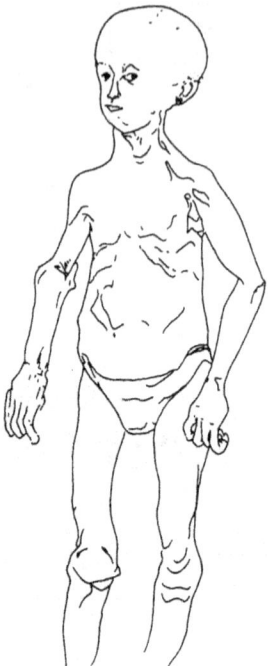

Fig. 6.13. Progeria.

Fig. 6.14. One way of calculating life expectancy!

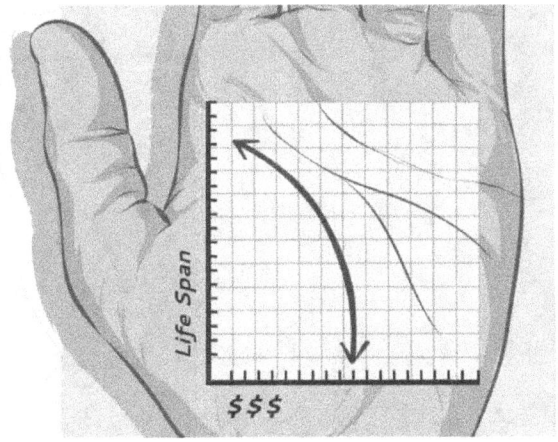

Fig. 6.15. Palm life line!

Gender differences in expectation of life at birth: 1950 - 2000

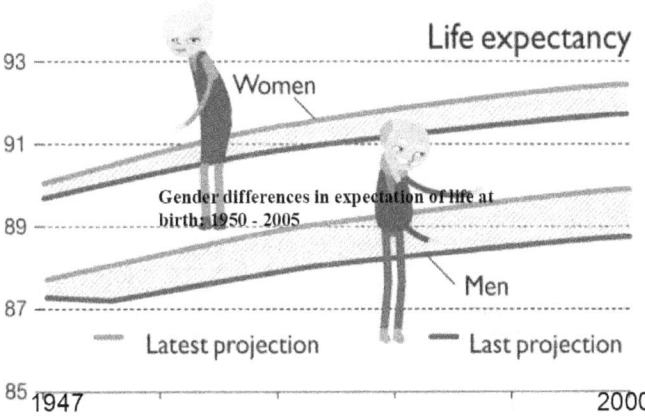

Fig. 6.16. Life expectancy by sex in humans.

Estimates assumed that life expectancy would level off (upper frame). But the lower frame (for Japan alone) shows that this did not happen!

But again, 2008 came and went. The second predicted levelling (Figure 6.24, upper frame) did not occur, see lower frame!

Again, 2008 came and went, but by 2020 the predicted levelling had still not occurred (Figure 6.25)! Which of the estimates

Fig. 6.17. How many little white haired old men can do this?

National differences in expectation of life at birth: 1950 - 2005

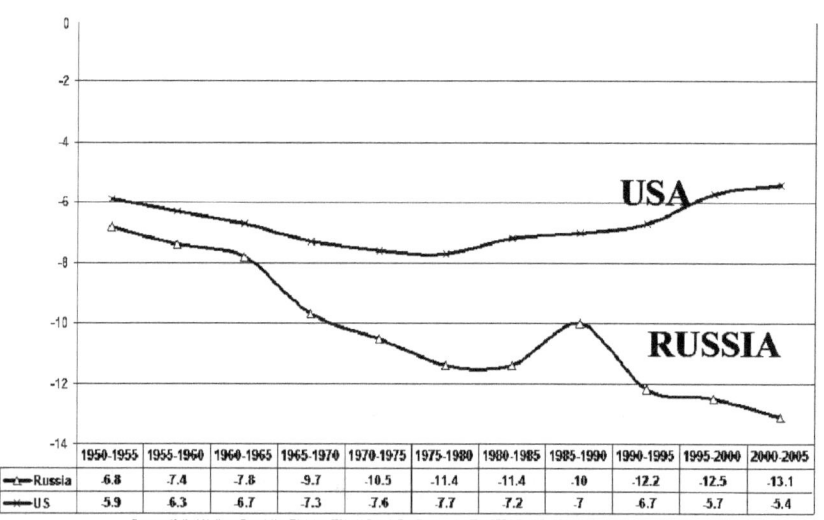

	1950-1955	1955-1960	1960-1965	1965-1970	1970-1975	1975-1980	1980-1985	1985-1990	1990-1995	1995-2000	2000-2005
Russia	-6.8	-7.4	-7.8	-9.7	-10.5	-11.4	-11.4	-10	-12.2	-12.5	-13.1
US	-5.9	-6.3	-6.7	-7.3	-7.6	-7.7	-7.2	-7	-6.7	-5.7	-5.4

Source: United Nations Population Division, "World Population Prospects: The 2004 Revision," http://esa.un.org/unpp/index.asp?panel=3

Fig. 6.18. An interesting national difference.

Aging and Death: Life Span, Mortality, Wellness and Illness! 131

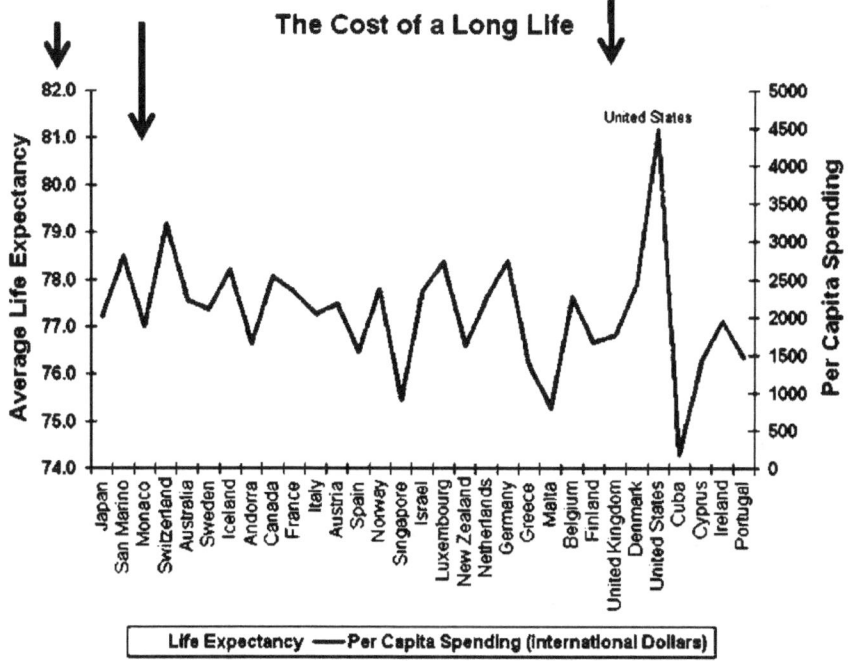

Fig. 6.19. The cost of a long life: the special case of the USA.

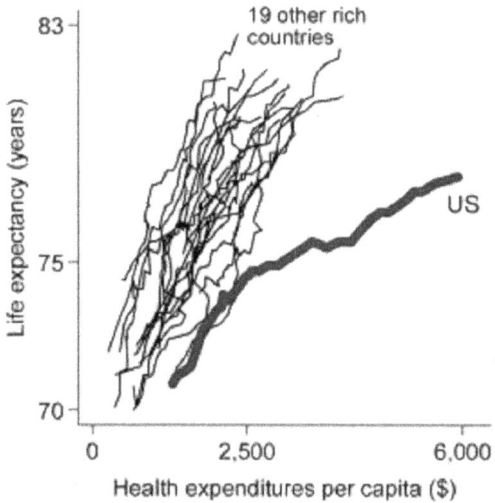

Life expectancy by health expenditures per capita, 1970-2008

Fig. 6.20. Again, the special case of the USA.

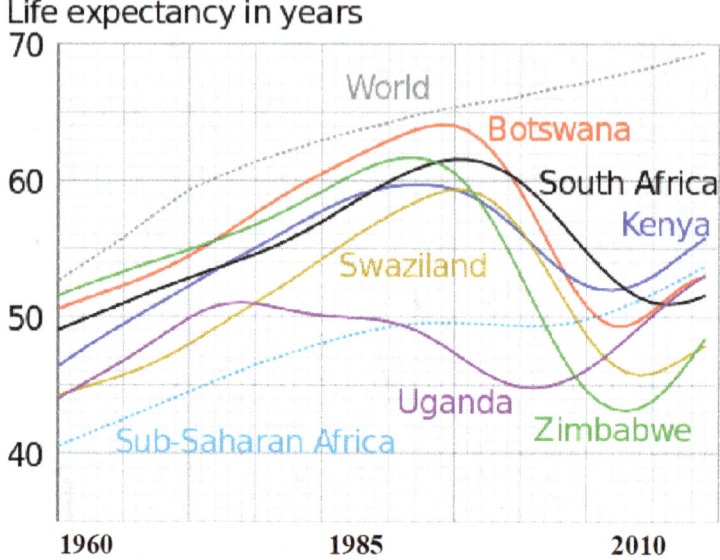

Fig. 6.21. A very sad picture.

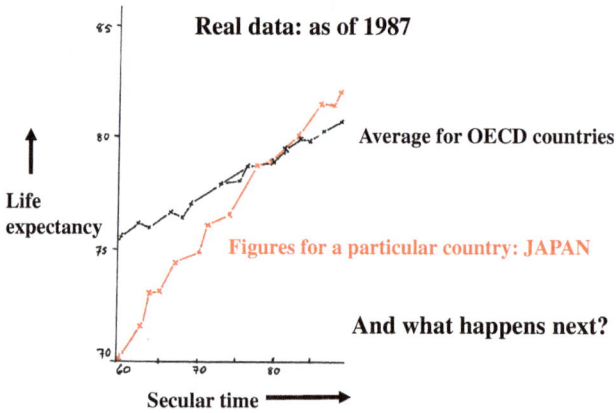

Fig. 6.22. Life expectancy for one particular country: Japan, in red, compared with the average for OECD countries.

from 2021 will eventuate for 2024 — a straight line still, or a levelling off? We will have to wait and see.

However, these last figures have become impacted by a very special situation. The tsunami that decimated parts of the

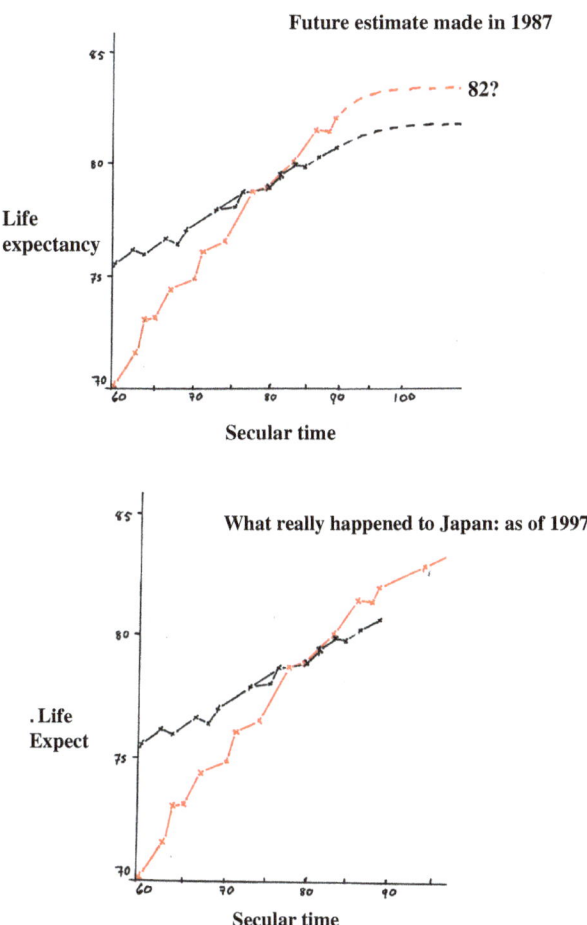

Fig. 6.23. The estimate for Japan made in 1987 (upper frame), and the reality actually occurring in 1997 (lower frame).

Japanese coastline destroyed an area with a large number of age-care buildings (and their aged occupants) located at that part of the coast. And the effects of Covid 19 deaths may be evident. The 2024 figures will be especially interesting.

All this leads to further questions. Will life expectancy really keep going up? Or will it eventually flatten out? What are the implications for the world, for our society, for us? We will go into

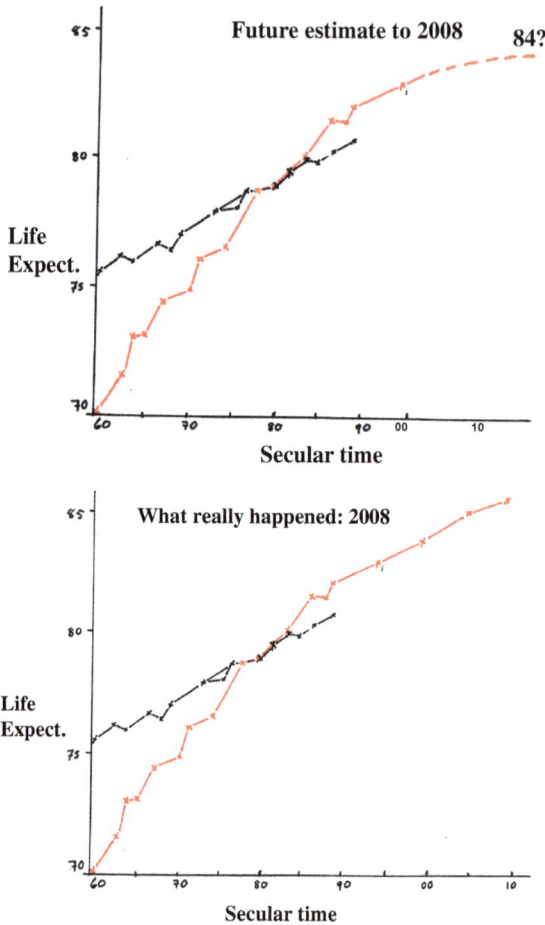

Fig. 6.24. The future estimate for Japan made in 2008 (upper frame) again expected levelling to occur, but the reality, lower frame, available at 2014, remained rising!

this matter after the next discussion of mortality. **We have been wrong so many times before!**

Human Mortality

Let us now look at mortality. Figure 6.26 shows the theory behind mortality — no longer an actuarial estimate, but the actual number of deaths in a population.

Aging and Death: Life Span, Mortality, Wellness and Illness! 135

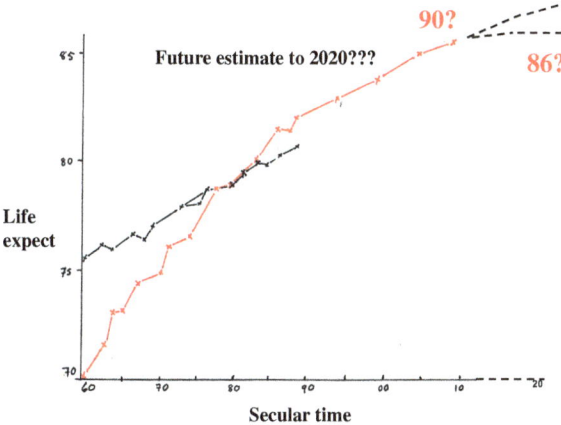

Fig. 6.25. Figures for 2020, estimates for 2024!

Now look at Mortality: theoretical curve for Mortality

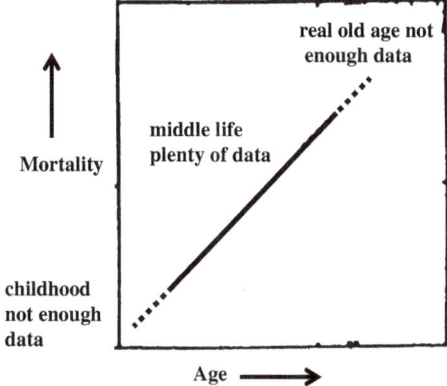

Fig. 6.26. The theory: mortality is a straight line, but there are so few deaths at the two ends, that the line for the very young and very old cannot really be calculated very accurately (hence dotted parts in the figure).

Let us now move from theory and examine some real data for mortality (Figure 6.27).

We can also examine what happens with larger and larger samples thus allowing better and better fitted lines (Figure 6.28).

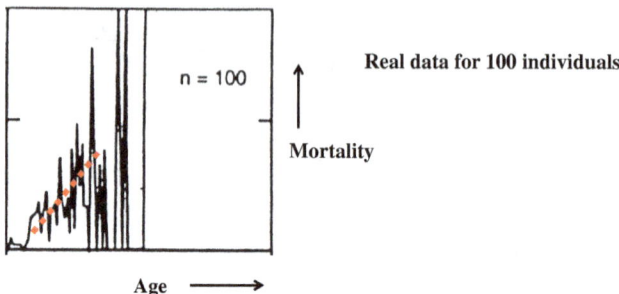

Fig. 6.27. Mortality for a single small sample.

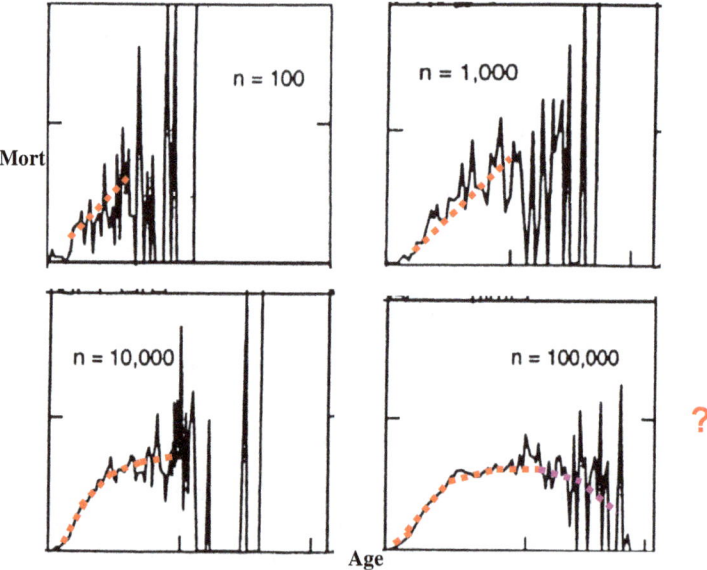

Fig. 6.28. With larger and larger samples, the initial straight-line plot gradually flattens out, and finally actually turns down!

Questions: Does mortality really stop being a straight line? Does mortality really start to fall? If it does, why? What are the implications for the world, for our society, for us?

Human populations have changed markedly over the years. From 1750 to 1950, the world's population grew from one billion to three billion. From 1950 to 2000, it grew from three billion to six billion. From 2000 to now, it is about nine billion. If this continues, the result may be catastrophic. Of course, a major nuclear accident, an unwillingness to give up fossil fuels, an inability to handle climate change, the entree of new and more dangerous pandemics, a China versus USA escalation of technology wars, or the real wars of Russia, and possibly, even, the possible wars of China to come, could be even more catastrophic (in very different ways).

Estimations of future changes have been made many times. H. G. Wells' (1933) guess for 2100 was sixteen billion (wrong). Hermann Kahn's estimate (1979) for 2100 was fifteen billion (wrong again). The United Nations have made several estimates over the years: including for 2050: eight billion, for 2075: seven billion, and (could this actually happen) at 2300, only four billion!

Only in the least developed world may populations really increase, e.g. until 2300, such as Congo or Bangladesh. Middle-tier countries may see populations stabilize at 2250, then possibly decline to 2300 — e.g. Brazil or South Korea. The most dramatic effect may be in advanced industrial countries: declines by 2250, with major declines by 2300.

Some estimated data for Australia made in 1975 included: 7.3 workers supporting each retiree by 1982, 6.6 workers for each retiree by 2021, 4.0 workers estimated for each retiree by 2240, and only 2.7 workers for each retiree by 2300! All of this has implications for lifestyles, economics, politics, nationalisms and religions: all possible new battle grounds!

If all this seems far-fetched, let us examine implications for individual lives.

Lifestyles: Measuring Individual Human Wellbeing

It is possible to think of the changes that occur in the life of each one of us. Geoffrey Harrison has provided us a model, using not real incidents, but possible incidents affecting overall wellbeing (Figure 6.29).

This model can then be applied for one day, youth, maturity, and old age (Figure 6.30).

At this point, however, we can look at new effects that modify the problems of the old. Is it possible that we have actually produced new difficulties for the old in our societies? These difficulties can be graphed as though their effects are to change the 100 percent limit for the old. This is implied in general terms in Figure 6.31. It is shown in detail in Figure 6.32.

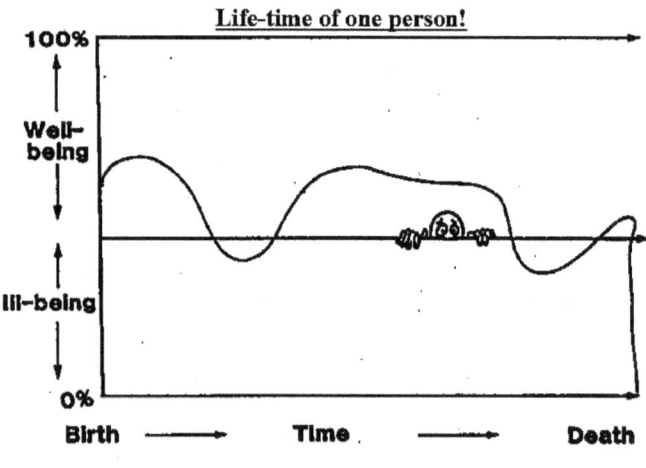

Harrison's model of change in well-being over time.

Fig. 6.29. The lifetime of one person.

Aging and Death: Life Span, Mortality, Wellness and Illness! 139

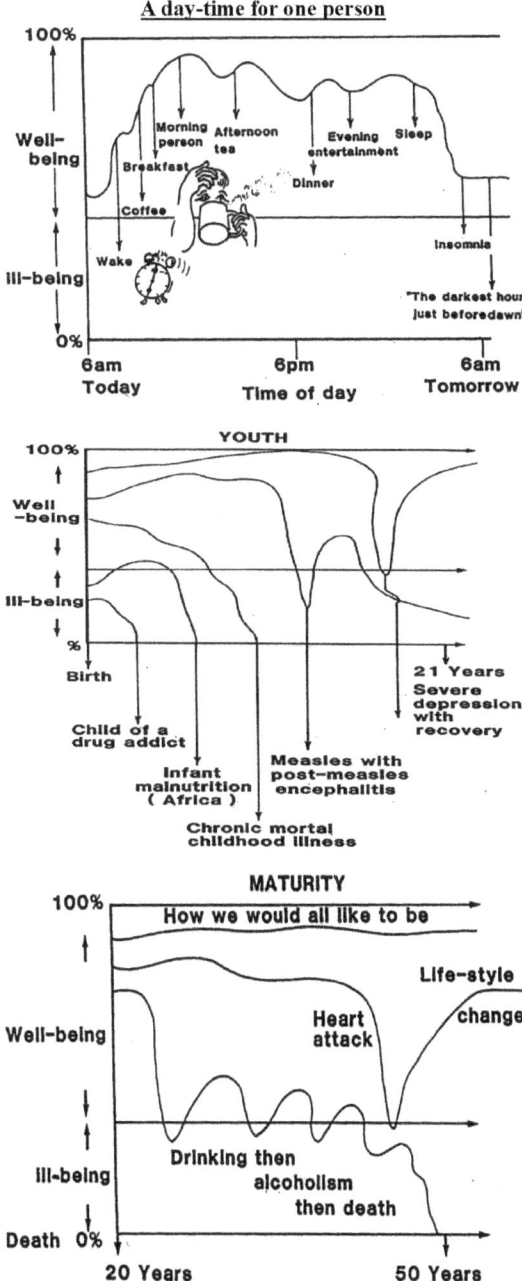

Fig. 6.30. Different curves for different ages.

140 *Humans and Change: Seven Ideas out of the Ordinary*

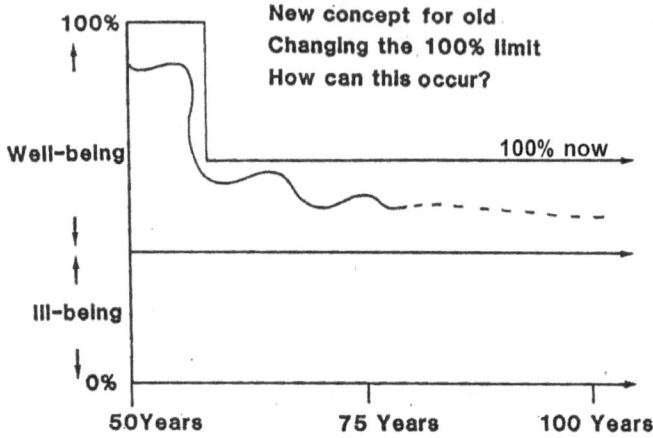

Fig. 6.31. The idea of changing the limit.

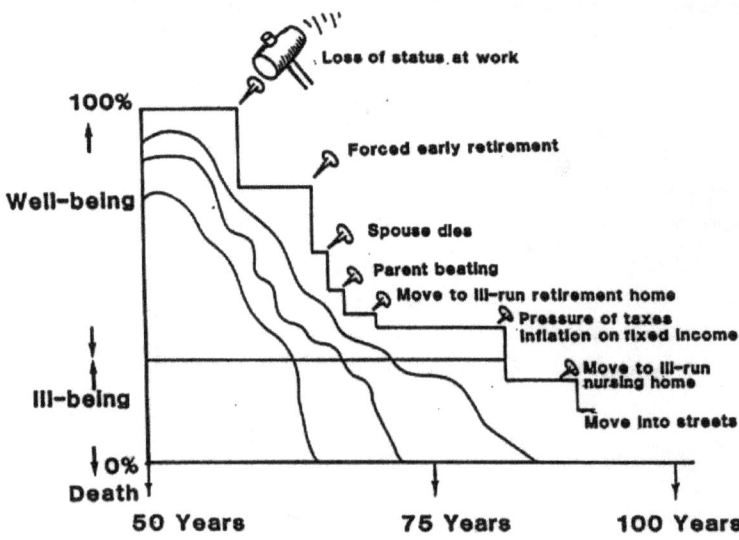

Fig. 6.32. Changing the limit: some realities.

This shows clearly how our communities, our organizations, and our governments not only fail to deal with aging, agism, and aging inequity, but make them worse.

Aging and the Brain

Finally, what about aging and the brain? Is it mostly almost over at age six (Figure 6.33)?

Yet this simple picture is actually much more complex. Thus, though overall brain volume changes little after six years of age, examination of more detailed structures show many more complex changes.

For example, the complexity of neural connections, from being sparse in the newborn, rises to a spike at two years, but then gradually falls in late childhood. It then rises again, coincident with puberty, then slowly falls again at later ages.

Again, for example, the development of synapses in various parts of the brain also vary enormously. It has its maximum for the functions of seeing and hearing at about six months of age, for language at about two years, for higher cognitive functions at four to six years.

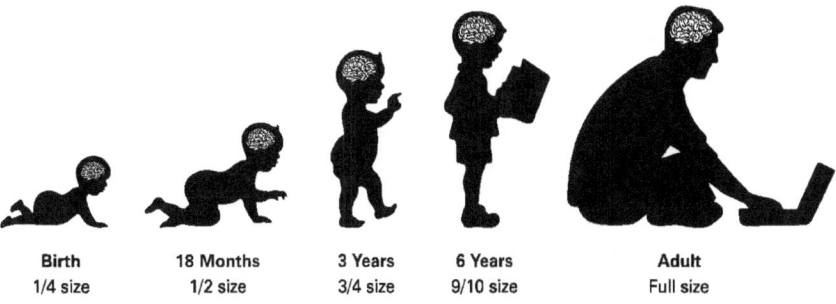

Fig. 6.33. For example, changes in brain volume do seem almost complete at six.

Yet again, while prefrontal excitatory synapses have their maximum at about two years, prefrontal inhibitory synapses max-out at twenty years. In contrast, prefrontal inhibitory synapses, quite low in childhood, rise to a maximum at fifteen and plateau in the 20s and 30s.

Are some of these data reflected in common or garden phrases like the wonderful 'wons', the 'sassy' sixes, the terrible 'teens', and so on?

These sequential changes during early growth lead on quite naturally to new ideas about human brain change.

Chapter 7
Human Brains: Not Just Bigger — Changed, Changing, Unique!

As do many workers in this area, I have my own story about the brain power of an animal. I was present when colleagues at Liverpool University were trying to use a force plate to obtain the foot pattern of a great ape walking on two legs (for comparison, of course, with fossil foot prints and the actual foot prints of today's humans). They had paid, I seem to remember, some several thousands of pounds for the force plate. It was placed in an area where the ape would walk. There was a hide where we could visualize, film and record what happened, all with permission, at Chester Zoo.

An Ape Anecdote

When the chimpanzee emerged from his covered quarters, he immediately realized there was something different. He looked carefully at the situation, walked around the force plate for a short time, but did not step on it. Then, perhaps assuming that there was nothing special in the situation (although who knows what he thought), he went off and paid no more attention to it. A gorilla gave the situation the same limited notice.

But with the orangutan, the story was different. He looked at the situation suspiciously, walked away, returned, looked at it again. He went away, returned again, looked at it very carefully, seemed to notice that one corner of the force plate was slightly raised, inserted a very powerful finger under this corner, pulled hard, pulled up the force plate, **and tore it in two!**

My colleagues, interested in the biomechanics of walking, really wanted this information, so more money was sprung for another force plate. This was duly installed rather more carefully. Again, the orangutan came out, again noticed something different, placed his finger down to attempt to raise the plate (but it had been better placed). No luck. So, after looking a little longer, he went away. Shortly after, he came back with a sack he had found elsewhere in the enclosure. He placed the edge of the sack under a still slightly protruding corner of the force plate, and with the extra leverage, pulled it up, **and again tore it apart.**

The orangutan seemed to have shown a degree of thought and foresight that had not occurred to the two other apes. I dearly wanted my colleagues to spring for a third force plate — to see what would happen — but they thought the cost was too great. Of course, this is only my own anecdote and probably doesn't mean anything much. But one could read it as an unusual level of thinking in that orangutan.

There was an interesting corollary to this ape anecdote, concerning a human. When we got back to the laboratory the second time, all my colleagues tried hard to tear the force plate, but they could not. They just did not have the power of the orangutan's hand and arm. The plate was then given to me, a relatively older, weaker, person, to try. My colleagues were absolutely amazed when I also tore the force plate across. Of course, they didn't know that I looked for a Griffith's crack in the force plate, and tried to tear it at that point. The apex of such a crack greatly increased the strain, magnifying my lesser power. (I do not believe the orangutan knew this!) What was going on in the brain of that orangutan?

From the Brain of that Orangutan to the Brains of all Primates

Thus, when biological aspects of the human body are examined, humans are indeed incredibly close to apes, monkeys, and even to most mammals of today: same flesh, same blood, same bone. Most anatomy, most physiology, most biochemistry, most genetics, tell us this. We are part of a continuum. And even when we look at fossils thought to be related to humans, the same finding, though it is just from bones, seems to be evident.

Likewise, when it comes to the human brain, the finding seems, superficially, to be more or less similar. Although brain size patterns differ among the various vertebrate classes (Figure 7.1),

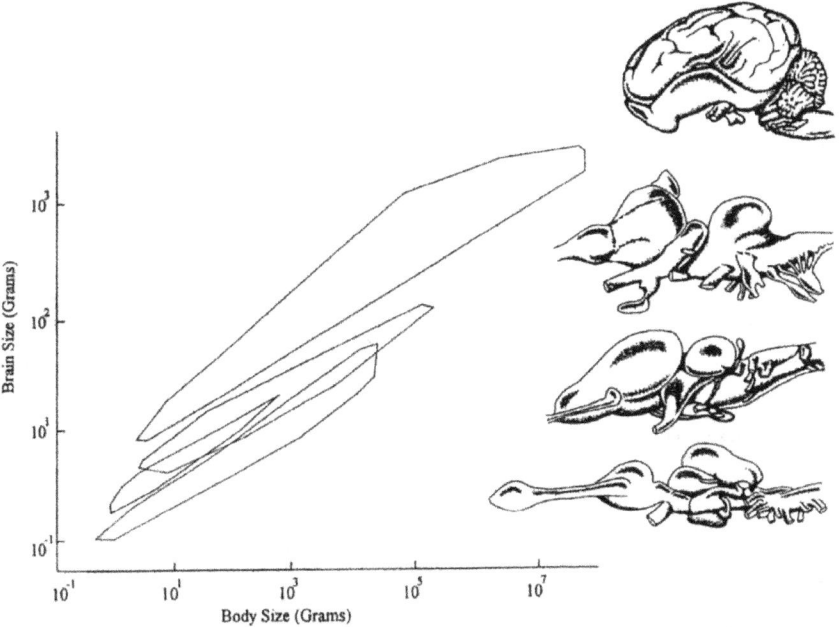

Fig. 7.1. Plots of brain sizes against body sizes in several different vertebrate classes, from mammals above, through birds, reptiles and fishes below, shows different brain/body relationships even though there are straight-line relationships within each vertebrate class.

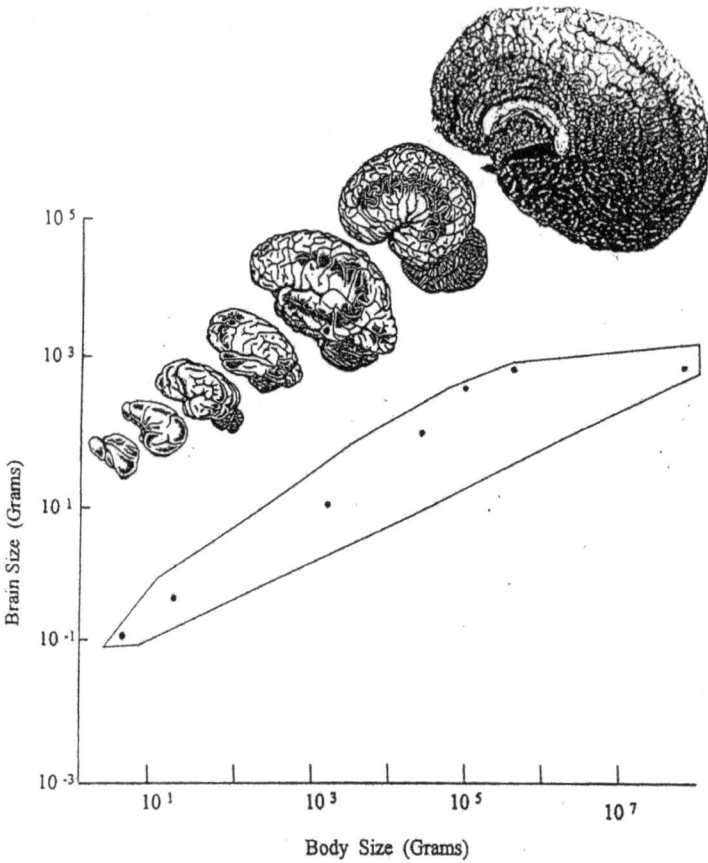

Fig. 7.2. Relationship between brain size and body size within primates (but including two very large creatures, 'honorary primates': dolphin and blue whale).

brain size patterns in primates seem similar in all primates, varying mainly only in relation to body size (Figure 7.2).

This is even so for humans, notwithstanding our relatively larger brains in relatively smaller bodies. We still fit approximately where one would expect. And even that large brain does not render us unique. Some creatures: dolphins, rorquals, elephants, whales, all very large animals, have yet very much larger brains still.

Likewise, the plot for primates alone shows a straight-line relationship (Figure 7.2).

There is only one almost straight-line relationship between brain size and body size. And there is nothing special about the place of humans. Humans seem to fit on the straight line! **Third Brain from the Top**! (That would make a good chapter or book title).

But, of course, these data are based upon absolute brain sizes alone. If we look at the picture based on brain size relative to skull length, then we see (upper diagonal row of Figure 7.3) what

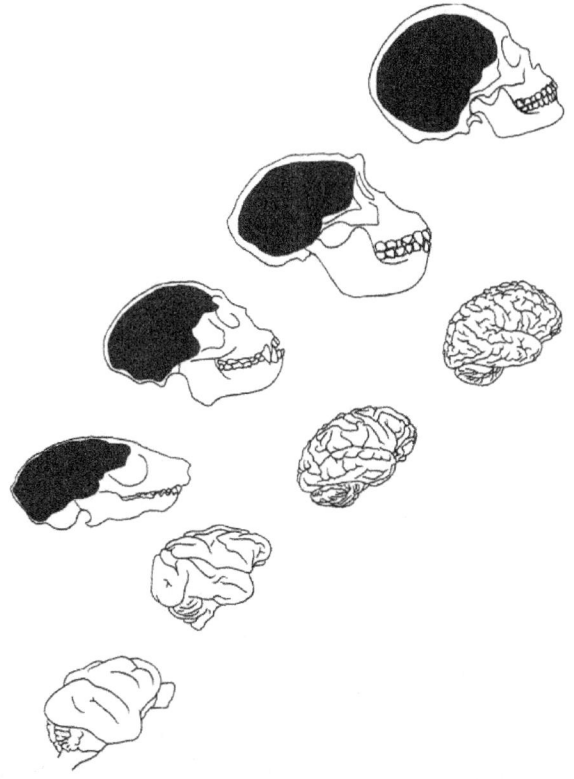

Fig. 7.3. The difference between brain size scaled against skull length (upper row) and brain complexity scaled against skull length (lower row).

everyone knows, that there is not that much difference among the species from prosimians, across monkeys and apes to humans.

In enormous contrast, however (lower diagonal row of Figure 7.3), drawings of cortical complexity relative to brain size or skull length (in those same specimens) show that there are enormous differences from prosimians, through monkeys, apes to humans in the complexity of visible brain sulci.

This picture should have forewarned me what was coming.

The Serendipity of Science

Not long after these ideas, in the late 1990s, a mature student (Willem de Winter) came to me with a serious problem. His supervisor had, unfortunately, just died. Willem was interested in behavior and the brain. The work was started. Would I be willing to help him finish his doctorate, which was on brain behavioral plasticity? I said I was very interested in his ideas, but that I generally preferred to test ideas with data and analyses.

Willem, in his turn, said he had become fascinated by our ways of handling measurements. He was especially excited when he found that our group had not only analyzed measurements of animal anatomies (which we had earlier called *'morphometrics'* and seemingly learnt something about animal morphology), but had also analyzed measurements of animal niches (with two colleagues, Robin Huw Crompton and Susan Sima Lieberman). We had called this work *'nichemetrics'* and seemingly learnt something about animal niches.

It seemed reasonable that such statistical analyses might be applied to data on brains, with the possibility of revealing something of brain workings (Willem's primary interest), and 'tongue in cheek' we would call it: *'neurometrics'*!

But where would we get measurements of brains?

It so happened that Heinz Stephan, of the Max Planck Institute, had measured the sizes of eleven brain parts, in more than 1,000 brains, in about 40 mammalian species of insectivores, bats and primates: 11,000 measurements overall. Stephan had only ever published, and subsequent workers only ever used, the data on the 40 species means.

Yet Stephan gave us the entire data set.
With our statistical methods of that time, we could analyze the
additional information,
(which no-one else had).

I must here record it as remarkable, even wonderful, that Heinz was willing to give Willem and I these data. Of course, he did not have the techniques that we were proposing to use; he could not have applied them himself. Nevertheless, it was still a remarkable *gift* (and one of several that I have received during my life, e.g. from Robin Crompton, David Johnston, Françoise Jouffroy, Peter Lisowski, Pan Ruliang, Adolph Schultz, and Wu Ru Kang, among many others).

Willem and I applied multivariate statistical methods to Stephan's individual brain part sizes. Willem wrote a significant thesis that melded both his original theoretical ideas on brain plasticity, and our applied suggestions on brain-part interrelationships. Ernst Mayr and George Williams were his two distinguished doctoral examiners; they rated his work 'highly commended'. This was even to the point (Mayr), of accepting Willem's criticisms of some of his (Mayr's) own prior opinions, (unusual acceptance indeed, but very welcome).

Of course, many other investigators had also analyzed Stephan's data, but only the data on species means, and using only the classical bivariate methods that were pretty much all that were generally available. But, relatively more recently, a few investigators had realized the value of using multivariate statistics. However, because the available data were only 'means of species', the only question they could ask, even with their particular multivariate statistic (Principal Components Analysis, PCA), was: *'How are the species means arranged?'* PCA, using the 'between the means' data matrix, could find that answer. The results were always simple. The means were always arranged along a straight line, and were 96 percent associated with overall body and brain size. The species with the smallest brains and bodies lay at one end of the linear array, those with the largest at the other.

Enough said, one would think! Yet our almost irreverent thought was:

"Surely these incredible data (certainly incredibly difficult to obtain) could tell us about more than just overall size!"

Could these extensive data really tell us nothing else?

Because Heinz gave us values for every specimen in every species (the full suite never published, and therefore not available to other workers), we could ask a different question:

How are the means between the species arranged?
When allowance is made for the variations among the specimens within the species?

This question requires a statistical method using both the 'between' and 'within' data matrices.

And we could ask that question in two ways:

We could ask it using *the simple **raw** sizes of brain parts*.
But we could also ask it using *the sizes of brain parts **relative** to one another.*

Analysis of 'raw brain part sizes', one would think, would give information mainly about 'raw brain size'. And this it did. So, it showed nothing new!

But analysis of 'relative brain part sizes' might be expected to relate, at least in part, to 'brain part relationships' and, perhaps, therefore, reflect *functional interactions* between brain parts.

Of course, we did both, but it was the 'relative brain part sizes' that showed a bold new picture.

As a first stab at the 'relative' problem, we looked at the size of each of brain part relative to the size of the main gateway (the medulla) between the body and the brain. We thought this might relate, to some extent at least, to nervous system traffic (**external talk**) between the body and the brain (except for the smaller portion of cranial nerve traffic bypassing the medulla). And it seemed to do so.

But we also thought that, perhaps, analysis of the internal ratios of the sizes of the different individual brain parts to one another, might reflect functional traffic (**internal cross-talk**) within the brain. So, we examined, for example, the size of the cerebellum relative to the cerebral cortex, the midbrain relative to the diencephalon, and so on.

In other words, we felt it possible that the *relative sizes* of parts to one another *within the brain* might reflect something of their *functional interactions*.

This is a crude idea compared to what could be done today with CAT scans, PET scans, MRIs, and many even newer techniques that can show not only detailed brain structure but even detailed brain function. But these expensive and time-consuming methods are mostly available only recently, and mostly only in medical contexts.

Who in this world could apply them to several tens of species, many hundreds of specimens, and many thousands of individual variables: the size of this data set? And where would they get the specimens and their brains? And would they have to be alive? So, crude though the brain part ratios were, they were all that were available, given the questions that we were asking. *And more importantly, these data had never been examined in this way.*

Of course, the proof of the pudding is in the results! The analysis of relationships from the raw brain part measurements lay on a straight line containing about 96 percent of the data. This is largely the same as the earlier literature studies. But the analysis of data comprising means and variances, both within and between species, showed that all primates were separated from all insectivores and all bats in different directions, save for an 'origin' where the groups intersected (Figure 7.4).

The whole result seems to be related to the major 'taxonomic' or 'evolutionary' separations between primates, insectivores, and bats! This was very clear, not all that surprising, and, frankly, not all that interesting (though it is of interest that all the smallest creatures, irrespective of major taxonomic group, were placed together, as though at an *origin!*).

> **But to our great surprise, deep within the study, we also found arrangements between particular groups of species that seemed explicable only on the grounds of functional (behavioral) parallels across taxonomic and/or evolutionary separations.**

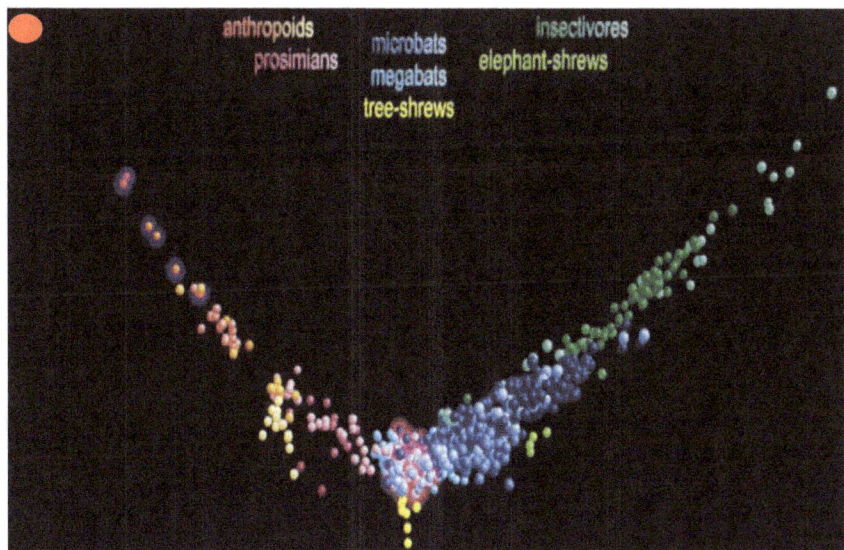

Fig. 7.4. Analysis of means and variances in primates (reds and yellows on the left), in insectivores (greens on the right), and bats (blues, lying centrally but actually projecting forwards out of the plane of the others. ***The large red dot, the human mean, is distinctive!***

For example, the fish-eating bats of the Old World fell with the fish-eating bats of the New World, rather than each with their own evolutionarily closer non-fish-eating bat relatives in 'each World'.

Again, for example, the burrowing 'moles' of both New World and Old World fell together, rather than each with their own evolutionarily closer non-burrowing relatives on their own continents.

Third, and of greatest interest to me, the most acrobatic New World monkeys (the woolly and spider monkeys) fell remarkably close to the most acrobatic Old World apes (orangutans, gibbons and siamangs). This was so, even though these New World and Old World species have been separated from each other, in evolutionary terms, for many millions of years.

We found more such functional parallels among other mammals.

Of course, these functional parallels are all obviously evident from body parts: large feet in flying fish-eaters, powerful forelimbs in burrowing mole-like creatures, long arms in arboreal acrobats. We might expect to find such body parallels in species with parallel behaviors, even though widely separated across both New and Old Worlds, ***if we were looking at the bodies of these creatures***.

Big feet are useful for fishing in all fish-eating bats, even if not closely related. Short but big and strong upper limbs are important in all burrowing animals whatever their evolutionary separations. Long arms might have evolved independently for arboreal activities in acrobatic apes and acrobatic New World monkeys, whatever their genetic heritage. All these are just classical functional parallels!

But we were not looking at their bodies. **We were looking at their brains!**

In other words, we had found fascinating equivalent parallels in internal brain organization. It is true that this was only at the crude, large brain part ratio level. It gave us a new idea, made us ask a new question: **could structures of relevant body parts really be associated with structures and functions of relevant brain parts?**

Most workers, perhaps blinded by the original 96 percent relationship of brain size with body size, had never examined this next step. They have assumed that brain sizes must result from body sizes, and stem from the known fundamental pattern of development and growth common to all mammals. They seem to have thought this was the primary, even sole, cause of these particular results?

However, there was more to come.

The Peculiar Position of the Human Brain

Humans lay on the same first axis as the other primates (Figure 7.5). But higher statistical axes (not separating any non-humans) further separated humans from all other primates to a very large degree (second and third frames).

This is such a large difference that we felt it necessary to identify the variables, that is, the various brain part ratios, responsible for it.

In the analysis of the first two axes, which placed humans as having just the largest brains, the ratios of importance were all those shown in the cartoon of Figure 7.6, that is: they were a series of hierarchical ratios between the lower hindbrain part (the medulla) and the upper midbrain and forebrain parts. It was these hierarchically related variables, that, when combined, separated humans from other primates by eight standard deviation units.

But examination of the other higher axes showed that the additional separation of humans from everything else was achieved in humans alone, by a series of networks of relationships between and among upper brain components alone (Figure 7.7).

And though these links included one single linked pair, they also included several three, or four, or even more parts linked together. This is a relationship more like a network, rather than a hierarchy.

This was not found among the non-human primates. Of course, this is not to say that there are **no networks** in non-human primates; there must be. But perhaps it says that networks are a much bigger proportion, a more obvious finding, for the human than the non-human brain.

Of course, these findings are based upon analysis of only these few, rather crude, brain part ratios. One can only guess how

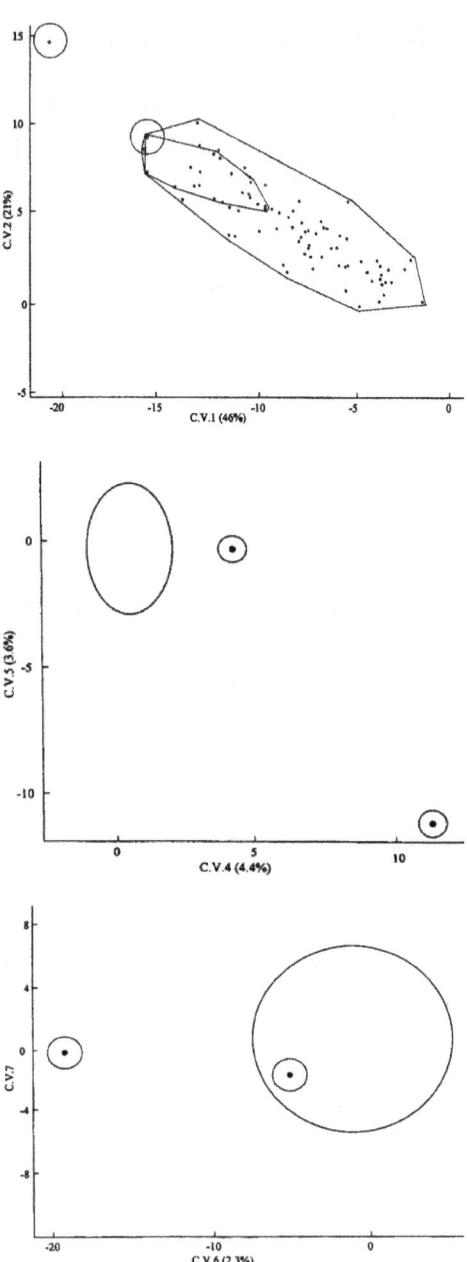

Fig. 7.5. The first frame shows 8 standard deviation units of difference in axes 1 and 2 of humans (top left small circle) from all other primates. But the lower 2 frames show further axes of the analysis (axes 4, 5, 6, and 7, scaled in standard deviation units) in which humans alone, the distant small ovals, are widely divergent from all other primates (large ovals) and chimpanzees (the other small ovals).

Human Brains: Not Just Bigger — Changed, Changing, Unique! 157

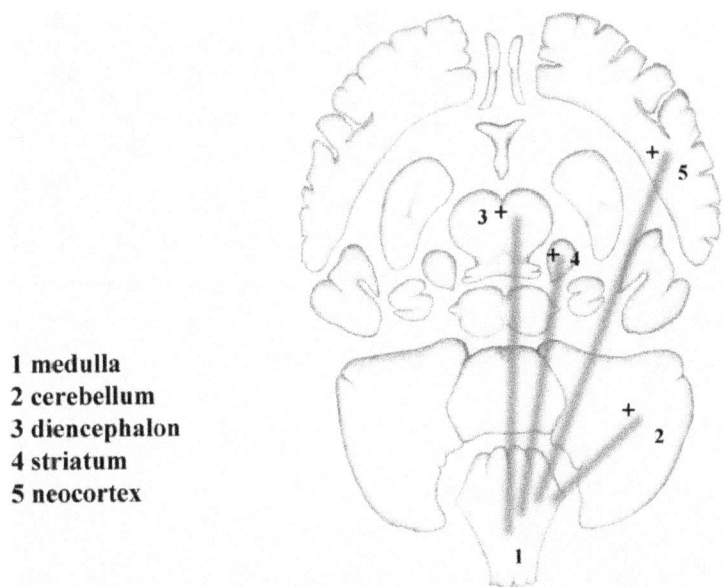

1 medulla
2 cerebellum
3 diencephalon
4 striatum
5 neocortex

Fig. 7.6. The 'hierarchical' links (simple linear links) between the lowest to higher brain part ratios that contribute most to the brain size separations of all primates.

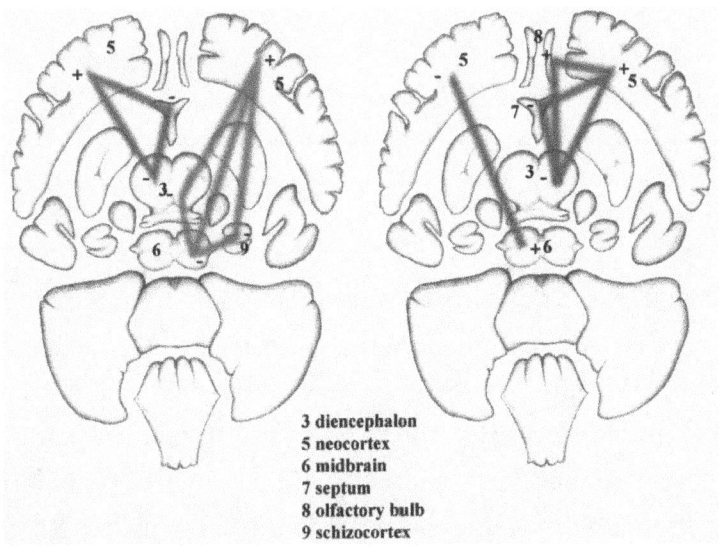

3 diencephalon
5 neocortex
6 midbrain
7 septum
8 olfactory bulb
9 schizocortex

Fig. 7.7. Two frames that show the internal 'network' links, mostly more complex triple and quadruple links, by which humans alone are separated from all other primates (including apes) by a total 22 standard deviation units!

much greater the separations might be if we had modern data (perhaps numbers of cells, or densities of connections, rather than just crude volumes), and data for the many other very important structures in the brain.

And if this guess about the increased importance of networks over hierarchies is correct, it might especially start to explain the nature of human uniqueness. Networks can have emergent properties far beyond those of hierarchies!

In other words, there seems to be a level of brain organization in humans (at this crude, large brain part level) that is much less evident in chimpanzees, or indeed, in any other non-human primate. Of course, a more fine-grained study would surely show the beginnings of this in other primates; it can't be unique to humans. The question is, however, what produces this special quantitative human separation?

It is not due to the hierarchies from lower medulla to higher mid- and forebrain brain parts that separate all primates.
It may be due to networks mostly within midbrain and forebrain parts and much more evident in humans than in other primates.

Given what I think are the enormous cognitive and behavioral differences between humans and non-humans, this seems entirely reasonable. Yet almost everyone else who has looked at brain sizes, blinded, perhaps, by the approximately 96 percent relationship with body size, and the equivalent 96 percent DNA similarity of humans and chimpanzees, have seen humans as just another ape. Indeed, we have even been called 'the third chimpanzee'.

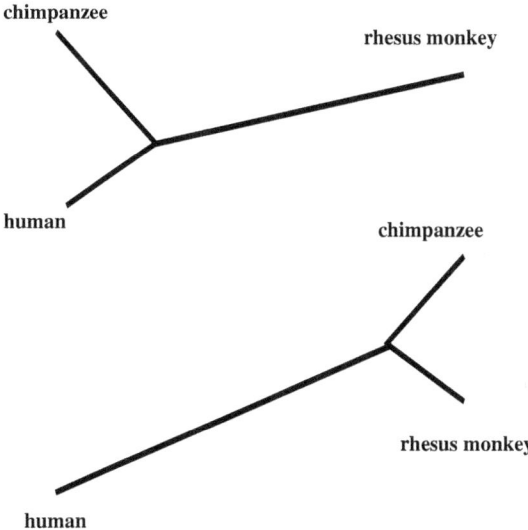

Fig. 7.8. Above: minimum spanning tree of relative distances between molecular factors for liver, kidney, blood and bone. Below: equivalent tree between molecular factors for brain!

How does this result for brains compare with investigations of other organs and tissues (Figure 7.8)?

Thus, most other organ molecular factors place the chimpanzee closer to the human (Figure 7.8, upper frame). In contrast, molecular factors for brain show chimpanzees closer to rhesus monkeys (Figure 7.8, lower frame). It is the second, brain–molecular relationship, to which our brain part ratio result seems more closely aligned (Figure 7.9).

Is it possible that, if studies allowed consideration of all interactions including between and within many smaller but critical brain parts, differences might be enormously greater still?

Is it also possible that these changes, though presumably starting gently, have been accelerating to greater and greater degrees in more recent evolutionary times?

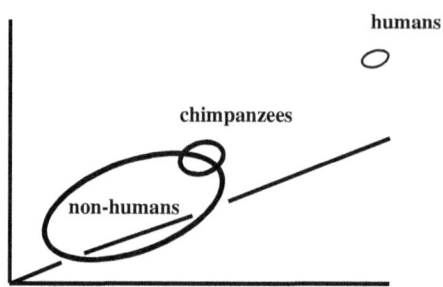

Fig. 7.9. The three-dimensional picture for plots of brain part ratios uniquely separates humans from all other primates. The scale of this diagram is such that the separation of humans from other primates, when all statistical axes are summed in a Pythagorean manner, is some 22 standard deviation units!

Are they, perhaps, accelerating fastest of all in the near past and even current times?

In times yet to come, could there be factors that might make them accelerate even more?

Would Looking at Close Fossil Relatives Help?

Although from the viewpoint of human evolution we have no measures of brain part sizes for the fossils (brains don't usually fossilize), we have surrogate measures for overall brain size in fossils: their endocranial volumes (Figures 7.10 and 7.11).

Apart from our inability to be certain from these figures whether the fossils are separate or overlapping groups, we can see one curious finding. One group, the Neanderthals, marked in red in Figure 7.11 actually relatively bigger than modern humans. Of course, this is well known.

But this leads to a further question. Could some of this be due simply to the problems of naming specimens and the overall paucity of fossils?

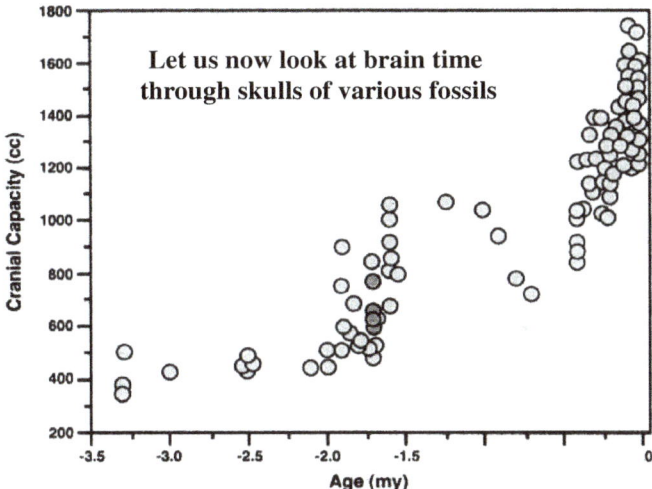

Fig. 7.10. The plot of hominin endocranial volumes over time.

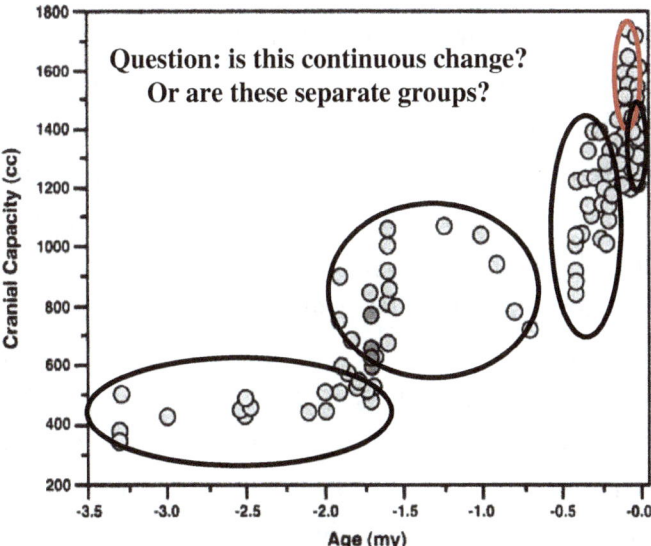

Fig. 7.11. With apparent groups identified, it is hard to know if the hominin brain size plot is a straight-line relationship or not!

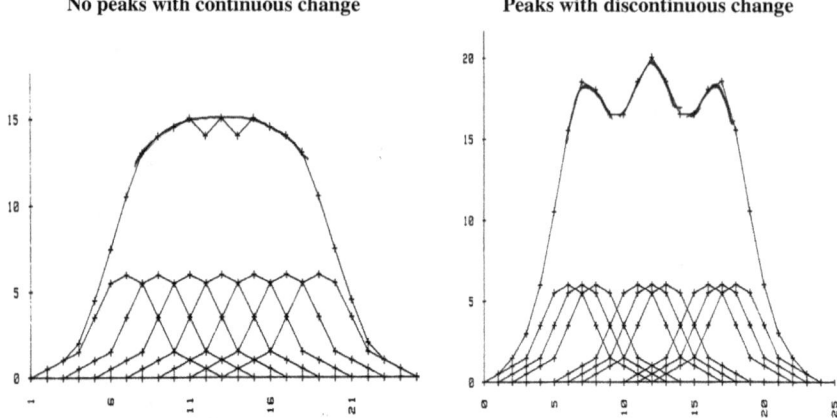

Fig. 7.12. The difference between continuous change and discontinuous change.

So, I tried first to see the difference between individual theoretical fossil specimens *a priori* using artificial data, and allowing groups, if any, to appear (Figure 7.12).

In other words, if there really are no groups, the overall curve should approximate a bell (like the left frame of Figure 7.12). If there really are separate groups, though the overall curve would still be a continuum, the individual peaks of the groups might well shine (ring) through (the bell), as in the right frame of Figure 7.12.

I then applied this theoretical idea to the real data, first analyzing the data in their named groups as defined by paleontology (Figure 7.13). The result: the statistical fits are not good!

I then analyzed the data without identifying the specimen groups (Figure 7.14). This second view, in contrast, shows some peaks, but not the peaks we might expect.

These data do not allow separation of australopithecines and habilines!
But they do allow identification of *erectus*!

They are somewhat equivocal about *sapiens* and *neanderthalensis* being separate; though they do indicate that the latter (only

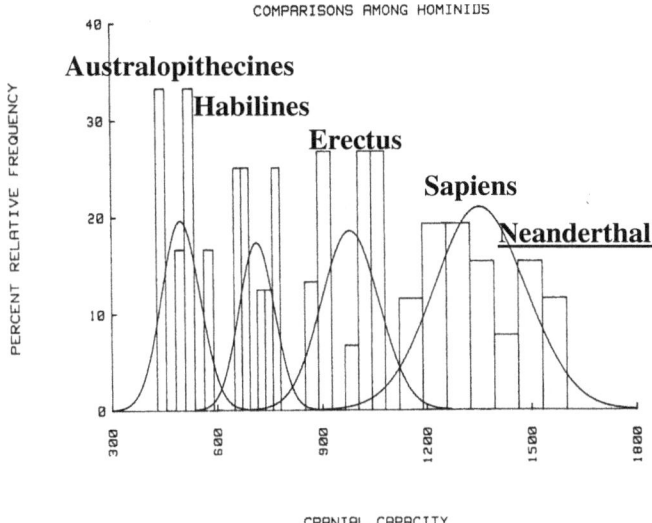

Fig. 7.13. The analysis with all groups identified, together with the normal curves plotted from the data; but, on a statistical basis, they are poor fits.

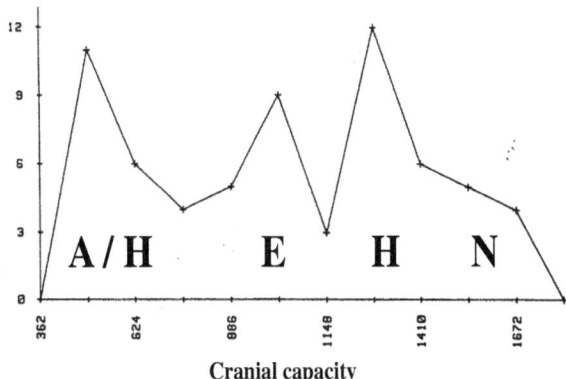

Fig. 7.14. The real relationships from Figure 7.13. The australopithecines and habilines (A/H) are not separately distinguishable (on the basis of these data). But erectus (E) is a single separate group. Modern humans (second H) and Neanderthalers (N) are not strongly statistically separate, although the Neanderthals, size-wise, are unequivocally clustered at the upper end of modern humans.

a few specimens) are bigger. Is it possible that the larger size of the Neanderthal brain and body fits with the size of ape brains and bodies, but that a relatively smaller human brain holds increased complexity?

Thus, the absolute sizes of both the modern human brain (in a human-sized body) and the Neanderthal brain (in a Neanderthal-sized body) fit reasonably well into a general primate pattern of simple brain size to body size. But their relative sizes suggest that modern humans are different from other primates in terms of internal complexity.

Will we ever know the true situation for Neanderthals?

The Implications?

When read superficially the latter picture is not a popular view.

Most morphologists see brains as the result **mainly** of common development and growth processes in primates as a whole, and there is some truth in this.

And in the same way, many behaviorists look to our various behaviors, for example our aggressions, our social structures, our creativities, even our mysticisms (there are many other such categories), as being closely related to prior non-human primate (even sometimes mammalian) equivalent characteristics. They are seen as close to, for example, ape aggressions, ape social structures, ape creativities, and precursors to ape mysticisms (whatever they might be). These seem to be the viewpoints of many who look to apes and monkeys, even other animals, for the determinants of presumed human equivalents. Again, there is considerable truth in this.

But this idea can be taken too far. Thus, human behaviors are usually portrayed, to use a geological metaphor, as:

> *a very thin veneer, or slice, or skin of human features, superimposed upon a very thick multilayered bedrock of complex ape and prior primate, even prior mammalian, characteristics.*

And that, therefore, this similarity is due to very close linear relationships,
and (possibly) a very short period of time.

But our analyses imply that modern human features are actually:

an enormously thick complex neural and cognitive multilaminar structure, overlying what is really only a thin sliver of bedrock of prior non-human characteristics.
This difference may therefore be due to a long period of separate change, particularly increasingly accelerating change, and development of increasingly complicated brain networks, evolving in ever more recent times.

The earliest thinkers saw, in many human behaviors, things that were nothing to do with apes and biological evolution, but were mainly socially determined.

Later workers saw in them the opposite: a simple extension of genetically and environmentally determined behaviors not too dissimilar from those of apes. They continued to emphasize this closeness of humans and apes, this similarity in the mechanisms. A few workers have even been willing to place humans and some apes in the same genus!

However, do these results not suggest that we should today recognize a more complex situation in humans? This is a situation that is the result, not just of a hierarchy of interactions from below upwards, but of whole new networks of interactions, between many complexly related cellular links, many genes, molecules, hormones and other chemistries, many environments (both biological and social), and many whole new networks of information transfer both within and between the generations.

Thus, behavioral work in apes has shown that some forms of networks do exist within local populations. They involve, for instance, copying within populations from individual to individual, among siblings and relatives, between parents and offspring. This occurs in most primates, and especially apes.

But a new form of networking can be achieved in humans by copying, not only within populations, but among outgroups, between generations, in some cases across many generations, and with temporal changes along the way. It requires materials, methods and links that do not occur to any major degree in non-humans, but that have been, and continue to be, and increasingly so, accelerating in timing and complexity in humans. This is in ways that are just not evident in other life forms.

This is 'education', in the broadest sense, not just the learning relationship from 'teacher' to 'student', nor even just among 'students' (both evident to a minor degree in non-human primates), but across several, even many, 'learning and teaching generations' in humans alone.

It is achieved by techniques whereby learning is not only passed on within families, but among communities, and over generations. It was aided at first by marks upon wet sand, then by knots on strings, impressions in clay tablets, carvings on stone and brick, inks on vellum and parchment, penned and later printed in books (this latter enormously accelerated by the invention of the pamphlet, the coffee house, the town crier, the reporter, and the printing press), and more recently still by yet other techniques: physical, electronic, in the cloud, and via artificial intelligence developments. 'Moore's Law' of technology may be having its special effect here. We will return to this idea later.

Human Brains Again: Are they Still Changing?

The very large complexity differences between human and ape brains that our analyses seem to show, and the newly increased amount of evolutionary time estimated on the basis of the molecules since their separation (see earlier), lead to another idea, another question. **Could it be that, in humans, changes in brain organization are partly due to new evolutionary mechanisms?**

This might produce very fast brain change, great elaboration of the brain function/behavior relationship, and both together suggesting totally new lifestyle possibilities. Is it at least possible that, though humans have smaller brains than Neanderthalers, the smaller brains contain more of the complex arrangements? The larger Neanderthaler brain, larger to go with the larger body, *though perhaps somewhat more like modern humans* (I must allow that possibility), may yet have been somewhat less complex, *somewhat more like other much earlier hominins, but probably rather different from the great apes.*

The new differences in human brain organization could stem in part from mechanisms for forming new connections much less available to other species. For example, increased levels of brain inputs and outputs are known to increase the number of dendrites and synapses within the rat brain. Of course, that kind of change is available to any species. But special effects in humans, **caused by ourselves**, and not possible in any but very minor degree in other species, could have especially affected the human brain.

Thus, the level of such effects in humans is enormously greater than in other species. For example, a singing, talking, touching (belly-caressing) pregnant woman and her partner, can have influences upon their fetus, and then later, their baby, then their child, as evidenced by changed patterns of movement of the late fetus, the neonate, the baby, even the only very young child, to sound, touch and sight. Even the fetus can 'hear'; note the well-known reactions of the fetus in 'utero', and of the post-natal baby. And this is even more true of the early child, reacting to happy or cross voices, to gentle or harsh sounds, especially to rhythm or discord, to caressing or hitting, even to different voices, even different languages!

Likewise, the influences of siblings, grandparents, and other close family and even friends, may have similar, if lesser, effects.

This does not easily occur, or occurs to much lesser degrees, in most other species, even the great apes.

Such influences in humans, beginning in later pregnancy, extending to infants and children, are therefore 'education' of a type. They cover not just formal education as we generally recognize it, but the 'education' that stems from all influences, even in a fetus and infant that, though it cannot yet speak, can vocalize, and can certainly see, hear, feel, and respond. For example, the late fetus actually responds, cringes even, to a new harsh, angry voice. Of course, in non-human primates, these initial influences presumably also exist. But they do not transpose into more complex, generation-crossing forms, as they do with the continuity of human 'education'.

Such effects not only modify the instructions of direct genetic factors, but also, through upstream and downstream effects, may actually change the results of the genetic instructions themselves. Ideas such as these were proposed theoretically by Waddington (The Epigenetic Landscape), by Moore (*The Dependent Gene*), and by Ridley (*Nature via Nurture*, not nature versus nurture).

Such changes may even relate to the findings by Fields about the functions of neuroglia, the special supportive cells that are far more numerous in human brains than in others.

Finally, there is even evidence that the new computer environment may produce, in humans, further new changes in the functions of brains, likely also in their structures, even their chemistries. And these may be passed on in time by mechanisms quite different from the usual (see below).

It is even not impossible that the earth for such change lies not only in **the addition of such newly recognized mechanisms**, but also in part in **the removal of some newly realized constraints** on brain structure and function.

The removal of these constraints stems from the relatively new evolution in humans of omnivory, and the removal, therefore, of the brain limiting effects of the mostly herbivorous, frugivorous, and folivorous diets of monkeys and apes (and presumably much earlier pre-humans) that result in lessened levels of essential amino acids, animal proteins, and cobalamins (this last especially in conjunction with negative effects of raised levels of folic acid in low cobalamin [vegetarian] diets).

Let us put these concepts into pictures. Waddington's metaphor helps give clarity. Waddington described development from the egg to the adult as the path that a ball takes rolling down a hill (Figure 7.15).

The position of the ball at the top represents the (genetic) beginning. As the ball rolls down the hill, it describes the pathway (epigenetic) of development and growth. This pathway depends upon both the starting position (beginning genetic information), and the contours of the hillside (the various downstream internal epigenetic and external environmental factors).

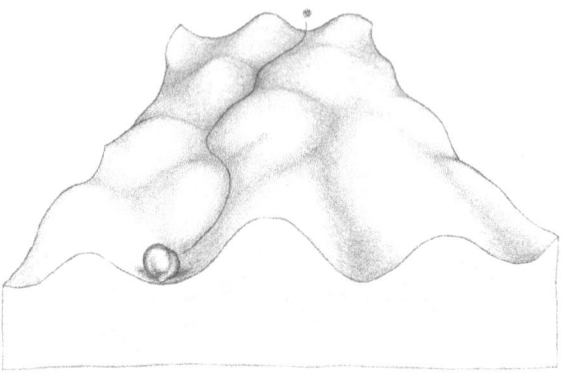

Fig. 7.15. Waddington's start from the gene in the zygote, along the epigenetic landscape, to an adult.

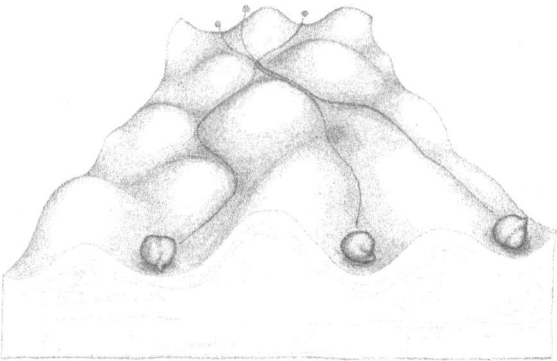

Fig. 7.16. Waddington's epigenetic pathway, showing how slightly different eggs may produce vastly different adults.

The final position of the ball at the bottom of the hill represents adult form and function.

With Waddington's metaphor in mind, let us examine the concept applied to a population. Thus, Figure 7.16 shows populations of genes. It diagrams how small, but nevertheless different, starting positions of the ball (small but important initial differences in genes) and gradually increasing changes in the landscape (increasing changes in the epigenetic factors) produce much larger adult differences.

Fig. 7.17. The epigenetic pathway, showing how small differences in embryos give rise to a larger difference in adults (upper frame), but also how separate small differences in two populations of embryos can give rise to larger differences between adults (lower frame).

There is nothing especially new here.

But the next figure (Figure 7.17, in reduced form), is explanatory in helping us to understand one way in which change can happen.

Let us now include the effect of changes in the landscape that are due to changes in contours *that are added **by the organism (humans) because it (we) can*** (Figure 7.18).

This changes a single group into two! Finally, however, we can envisage a situation where a generation can be changed by

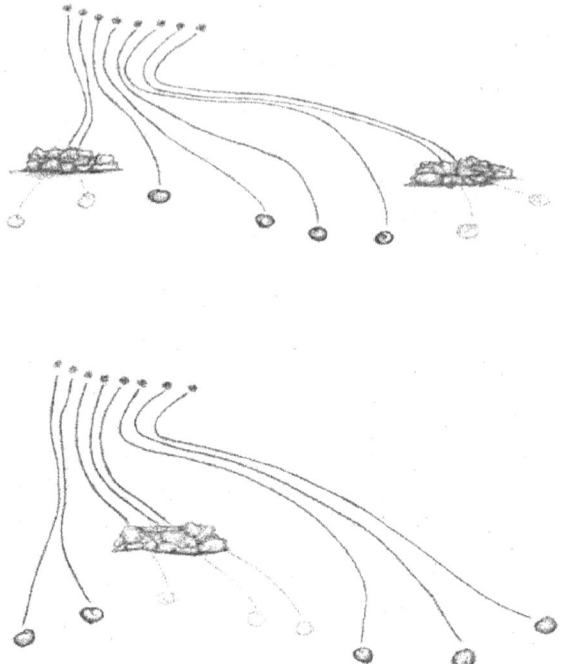

Fig. 7.18. Upper frame: two blocks in the landscape narrow the variation of a single group of adults. Lower frame: one block, in the right place, creates two separate types of adults.

changing the timing, blocking the landscape earlier and earlier. The effect of late change (Figure 7.19) can be increased by a similar but earlier change.

This change could produce another new and even greater separation of adults, effected *by a population on its descendants because it can, by introducing education earlier and earlier.*

Such 'educational' changes could include: (a) the (now standard) effects of the interactions between the genetic factors themselves and the various internal upstream and downstream molecular factors. But they could also include: (b) the effects of education from the new information technology mechanisms, including, now, artificial intelligence restricted to humans. They

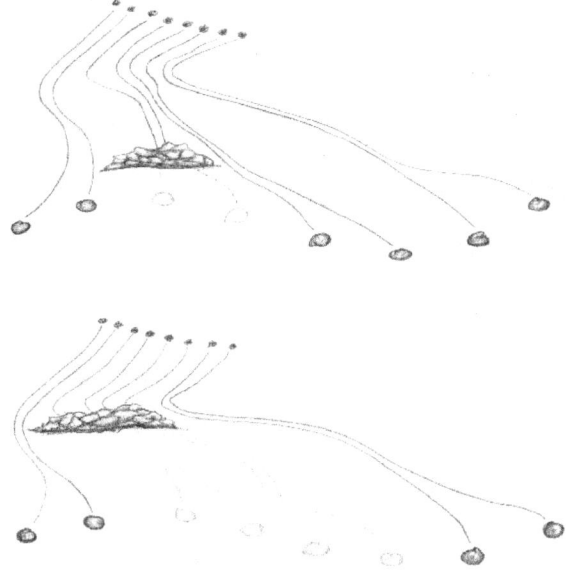

Fig. 7.19. Upper frame: creating two groups by an epigenetic effect in timing, eliminating some central individuals. Lower frame: greatly increased group separation by an earlier epigenetic effect (earlier 'education') keeping extreme individuals while eliminating centrals.

also could be due to: (c) the increased complexity of synapses, (d) the complexity-increasing effects of a much greater volume of glia (if that concept is eventually proven), (e) the removal of animal protein deficiency and cyanocobalamin constraining limitations on brain development, and (f) increasing changes in ever shorter periods of time (including changes into the future [our future]). But, perhaps most of all, they could include (g): the various interactions that may occur between all these different influencing modalities.

Figure 7.19 further implies that the effect of all these factors might not only produce new forms for some adults, *but also eliminate some adults that would otherwise have been produced.* Though, of course, those genomes that pass through remain the same, one would not expect this to produce evolution in the direct sense. It could result, however, in a well-known situation that might nevertheless engender very fast change. That is: such a system might give rise to greatly speeded reproductive isolation. Given the normal breeding propensities of humans this would seem, on the face of it, to be unlikely. However, let us go further.

This idea is the reverse of some educational theories current at the present day (i.e. education starting later and later, often not until the ages of six or even seven in parts of the USA, even no education at all for some individuals — especially women — in some societies today). But it fits with some educational systems of the past, e.g. education in Scotland starting as early as 3–4 years old. The Scottish teacher in my day was alarmed if her (sic) first task was to teach the child to read. It was expected that the child had learned to read at its mother's (sic) knee. The teacher's first job was to teach the child to write and figure! Even so, the ordinary forms of education, with which we are all familiar, are unlikely to produce sexual isolation in this way.

But new forms of education (hinted at above) are most obvious today in the use of the computer and the iPad, of the new information technology, even the most recent artificial intelligence systems applied at increasingly younger ages. (We have even seen the baby in the pram kept quiet by its own *seemingly meaningful* manipulation of its parent's iPhone, or even its own mini-tablet, the new pacifier.) The application of all this to increasingly limited portions of the population, just might produce unexpected brain change in early development.

Who amongst us has not been embarrassed by the teen, even the child, almost the infant, who knows how to 'work the machine', and who is scathing that nanny and grandad ('nain' and 'taid', especially 'hen nain' and 'hen daid') can't? It is just possible that information technology may be doing something very interesting to the brains of information-generations of developing humans.

Certainly I, myself, became aware, at a particular point in time, of the brain-changing effects of the excessive use of a particular computer game. Starting with 'wins' of a few hundred points, I progressed to as far as 27,000 points! Was there no end to my abilities? But then I developed moving images of the game when I was not playing, when I had my eyes closed, and I could even 'see' it in dreams remembered on awakening! I gave up in a fright! Would that I could have cut up my own brain to find out what was happening! Or perhaps non-invasive imaging methods might have told me.

Human Brains a Third Time: More Changes

To return to the main thesis, certainly, changes like these have been occurring more and more quickly over ever shorter and shorter periods of time. And the latest developments might give rise to changes in the human brain in quite new ways.

Some of these are relatively simple to understand, even if very difficult to correct. The psychological damages done to children, teenagers, even young adults, by 'online bullying', by availability of inappropriate social, sexual, and mental tortures, sometimes even leading to suicides from 'online' activities.

Other effects may turn out to be more complex and have not been fully worked out. I refer here to the new developments of computers, tablets, iPhones and the cloud. Such further effects relate to what humans can think and do. Thus, while these technologies can enhance certain aspects of education, they can damage others, especially personal growth in writing, reading, figuring and creating, all apparently not needed when the 'machine' can do it for you, hence the recent sophistication of cheating!

But they also seem to have functional-structural effects upon organic brain components, changing the numbers of cells, the amounts of connectivity, even the choices of brain pathways, all at speeds far greater than is found in evolutionary change. I refer here particularly to possible effects of the development of artificial intelligence (AI). Of course, on the positive side, AI has the capacity to take the drudgery out of work, allowing humans to think and be more creative. On the opposite side, one effect might be developments negatively affecting work, on people's labor, and therefore on people's lives, taking over much of life's activities, leaving little that is creative to people.

But even further is the possibility, actually already the reality, that stems from artificial intelligence. Thus, in addition to what AI can do to us (both positive and negative), AI is now starting to be able to do something to itself, generating a next variation of artificial intelligence. This, in turn, may generate a third. Sequential later generations of AI may be able to occur without human intervention (Machine Generations of AI, MGAI). Of course, in a first iteration such changes might be very small, might not even be noticed. But they might well go on, in larger and larger steps, creating subsequent machine generations: Mark two MGAI, Mark three MGAI ... Mark many MGAIs.

Continuation of such a process could eventually result in a new AI (perhaps a Total Machine AI, TMAI), acting in directions over which humans have absolutely no control. It is not impossible that this could spiral into what might be called, SHTMAI (Super Human Total Machine Artificial Intelligence), or (tongue in cheek) possibly even GAI (God AI)!

Such developments sound fearful, almost ridiculous. But they are not impossible. For example, such AI systems, designed to do certain things, could run away doing other things, even if the eventual result were negative for humanity.

Could this be how the world ends, not with a bang but a whimper?

But it is also not impossible that they might be increasingly good for humanity as long as humanity learns how to live with them, and channel them in appropriate ways.

Am I certain that this can be achieved?
Our inability to cope with iPhone bullying and misinformation do not make me optimistic!

The benefits that could accrue to humanity with socially positive applications of AI and its descendants could be great. But these powerful tools could have very negative uses, such uses could accrue very quickly, and society does not seem to be ready to deal with them.

Humanity has had so little success in handling its current problems: inequities, sexisms, racisms, outsiders, enemies, and so on, that I do not have great optimism about these new, mainly future, problems. But maybe that's because my end, too, is Nye!

A Special Summary for Brain Changes

Thus, in summary, many possibilities for brain change might produce developmental damages (changes) in the brain in individuals, especially early from infancy through to beginning adulthood. Such effects might be strongly negative. We already hear voices warning about the dangers of computers to the brains of the young. Uncontrolled access to computers and related gadgets by the young might well be strongly deleterious. The resultant *Homo nerdensis* might be a developmental liability!

Yet some such changes might be extremely powerfully positive, resulting in *Homo sapientior*. (Name suggestion thanks to discussions with a colleague in classics together with neurobiologist, Alan Harvey.) This might affect humanity in a different way. For example, I doubt that *Homo nerdensis* would very often breed with non-*nerdensis* forms. *Homo nerdensis* seems so often to suffer from such major behavioral problems in getting on with others that breeding *in toto* might well be reduced or might even not occur; (but tongue-in-cheek here, who knows what sex can do!).

Thus, female *Homo sapientior* may well seek out only her own! Already improvements in women's education in some countries seem to be associated with women tending, more and more, to seek out only men who are educated at their own level *or above*. Are 'lesser' males being removed from the breeding pools of these 'super' women? Are we seeing this in the flurries of unmarried men (*Guang Gun:* bare branches, no wives) and unmarried women (*Sheng Nu:* leftover women) in China; in the lonely males (*Hikikomori* boys and *Otaku* men) of Japan; even in the *NEETs* (Not in Education Employment or Training, who are largely male) of Britain and Europe?

Are there really a number of new possibilities for change in the human brain, and therefore in humans? Was Aldous Huxley (1946) correct in imagining his Alpha intellectuals (given extra stimulation) and his Delta minuses (the equivalent of today's progeny of the drinking pregnant mum)? Was Julian Huxley (1957) correct in envisioning a new taxonomic group, the *Psychozoa*, containing, at this point, only humans? Was H. G. Wells (both himself, 1895, and his alter ego, David Lake, 1981) percipient in seeing *Eloi* and *Morlocks* in our human future?

Could *Homo* split (again tongue in cheek)? Wow, what a heresy!

That Brain Heresy!

The idea of heresy became especially evident as Willem and I tried to publish our first paper on the brain. *Nature* turned the manuscript down 'in house' (i.e. not externally refereed). This is not unusual; *Nature* is flooded with great numbers of articles, many of them are very good, not all can be taken! One accepts this kind of rebuff gracefully. It happens to all of us, and to me, many times!

However, not too long after that rejection, another paper appeared in *Nature*. It was based only on the means of the species (the published and therefore freely available data) of Stephan. That paper had carried out a somewhat similar study as ours, but only on the between-the-species-means separations. It contained some of the ideas in our rejected paper. But it had not identified the enormous separation of humans (at that stage we had not overly emphasized that finding in our submission).

How had that paper been published when our own far more sophisticated analysis on both species statistics and individual statistics was rejected?

I thought about this and persuaded Willem that we should have another try at *Nature*. We submitted what we thought was an improved paper and especially referred to the new *Nature* paper published since our first try. This time, again, ours was turned down ('in house', in only 24 hours!).

I thought yet further about this, and after taking soundings from neurobiological colleagues (remember, I am not, myself, a neurobiologist!), I decided to write personally to the editor of *Nature* about the decision. This is the sort of correspondence that *Nature* generally doesn't enter into. It was certainly, something that I would not lightly do. I was very, very polite. But perhaps the editor realized that, in these consecutive turn-downs, and with the advice of neuroanatomical colleagues, I had 'smelt a rat'.

We were, therefore, surprised but enormously pleased, to be invited to present a yet further revision. Which we did. **And this version Nature published!**

Now I have had some ten or so papers in *Nature* over the years (this is not boasting; ten papers are not actually many when seen in the light of, at that point, a fifty-year career). But it must be unusual for *Nature* to publish after three turn-downs!

It reminded me of the problems I had had with *Nature* in publishing on a previous occasion when I was presenting an idea with the title: *Australopithecine fossils: grounds for doubt*. That paper too, was not liked by the then conventional wisdom who had no doubts! It too, was initially turned down. It took considerable pressure for it to be published (although in this case, *a female editor of Nature* was on my side!).

This leads me to think that, perhaps, today, it is the time to recognize more complex possibilities for the brain. To recognize that the brain and its mind are the result, not just of genetics and environment and their interaction, not just of behavioral copying and its interactions, but of the special abilities of humans to pass on information and new ideas, in many different modes, over long periods of time.

This involves not only copying from individual to individual, including from parents to offspring, teachers to students (both occur in many animals), but also the special ability for transmission across several, even many, generations. Such transmissions occur by means of materials and methods that have not only become orders of magnitude different from anything evident in non-humans, but that have been, and continue to be, and increasingly so, changing, in ways that are new even for today.

This is 'education', not just 'copying' from 'teacher' to 'student' or between 'students', (sometimes even from 'student' to 'teacher'), and not just within one educational generation, but across several, even many, generations. This latter is permitted by a variety of methods, from scratches in the sand, carving on wood or stone, knots in string, marks on vellum, writing on paper, printing with moveable type, passing information by semaphore and braille, by electrical, telephonic, wireless (radio), and finally by more modern developments: from paper tape, through IBM cards, memory sticks, the desktop, the cloud, artificial intelligence, to, for some, the quantum computer.

The effect of all of these mechanisms of education, even the most lowly of them, even as many as thousands of years ago, at first very slowly, but gradually becoming faster and faster, is that 'education' has been changing. And it has been changing at ever increasing speeds, and changing, as it goes, the human brain and its mind.

These are changes whereby learning is passed across the groups and over the generations, not only in hierarchies but through networks, and with both physical and electronic materials. 'Moore's Law' of technology may be having its special effect on the brain and mind.

What are the implications for humans today? And for those who would like to study them?

Chapter 8
Progress of Ideas: Challenge, Threat and Glory?

It was once the case that young students, teachers, researchers, would aspire to be professors, even distinguished professors, in the chosen parts of their subjects. They would not only want to teach what was already known, but find new knowledge, and want to improve their disciplines. And most of all, they would wish for new and better students to carry on the flame. These were some of their aims.

Today all that has changed.

Professors today are rarely able to do these things. They are overly burdened with lower-level administration, carrying out the dictates of higher-level administrators. They can no longer develop their disciplines through appointments and promotions of younger colleagues. Their tasks now are to 'dis-appoint' and 'de-promote'. They do not have the time, or the brief, or the support, to have much effect upon their disciplinary development (one of their major functions in my day). About all that they can now do is appoint temporary part-time assistant teachers and researchers, in lieu of lost full-timers!

These changes have come about as the decisions (powers) have moved from academia to administration, from the mores of collegiality to the customs of business! But this is not totally the fault of administrators. They, in their turn, are the minions of government. It is government that does not value teaching and learning, schools and universities, testing old ideas and creating new ones.

As a result, universities are, once again, suffering a brain drain, but one different from the brain drain of my youth. In my youth, the UK brain drain was a pull from overseas, a pull by overseas funds, overseas facilities and overseas careers (especially, at that time, by the USA). Today, the brain drain is almost the opposite; a push, almost deliberate, by government and officialdom from research and teaching here, to almost anything and anywhere else!

Eight of my recent students, all good students, have been so pushed away. Some of them were among the best I have had.

One obtained two PhDs, a first in theoretical plasma physics, and a second, with me, in mathematical biology. He got his second PhD with honors, something awarded to less than five percent of doctorates (at UWA). But a subsequent **secure research and teaching position could not be obtained,** either with me, or elsewhere. He was eventually forced to become, for a number of years, a mainstay of computing in the banking world (and made money!). After that he did manage to return to his love of teaching, but as a high-level teacher of STEM subjects in a high school. Of course, this *cursus honorum* was first good for the bank, later very good for the high school. But it was a major loss for the university, for his discipline, for finding new knowledge, *and for his psyche*!

Another of my post-PhD researchers, because the university did not have the funds to give her a long-term career (she wasn't even asking for more money, **she was just a researcher and a mother seeking security**), was driven to a major research position with millions of research dollars in a top laboratory in the USA (with Novartis, as it happens, the London home of which I had known in earlier days). At least the women full-professors in my area were *black affronted* by this case. But it did no good.

> *The administration*
> *would not relent;*
> *she went.*

A third young researcher, absolutely fascinated by the work she was doing, just could not get a secure university position, only a series of part-time temporary teaching posts. These kept her doing some research, but not at full blast. She stuck it out for several years, hoping! But eventually she decided that "discretion etc. ...", and she took a teaching diploma. She now has a high-level position in a high school, helping to encourage and prepare students (many of them indigenous) who have abilities but need aspiration, to think of further and higher education. This is a 'partial win' for her, of course. And it is a 'major win' for those indigenous students and for that high school. Even possibly, it is a 'win' in the long term for education. But would the result have been even better if she had been able to continue fully in university research and teaching? Possibly yes; possibly no! We will never know. But what I do know is that

an excellent investigator was denied the career she wanted, and for which she was properly prepared.

And there was *great angst in making the change!*

There are now many more women being appointed in academia. *And this is appropriate.* But more and more, these new appointments are part-time, or temporary, or short-term, and usually less well paid! This is not good for women. And not good for men who have already voted with their feet. The older men have already gone, the younger ones are generally not coming, *and the secure positions have disappeared*!

Security in university can only be achieved today by leaving insecure part-time research or insecure part-time teaching, and moving to administration. Jobs in administration can lead to, not tenure, but at least ongoing appointments with promotional possibilities; (for example: to school administrator, faculty secretary, postgraduate dean, research provost, deputy vice-chancellor, and for a few, the top prize, principal, president or vice-chancellor).

Of course, by then they have long been lost from research and teaching!

Times have changed from the days when professors, as a group, influenced the academic direction of the university by advising vice-chancellors. Academic boards are now largely paper tigers! They have few useful effects upon university directions. And thank goodness that is so, say many current administrators, for whom academic boards and their professors are a nuisance (except when manipulated as paper tigers).

We are now in a time when central administrators manage the top professors, and governments manage the central administrators, both based on the holding of the purse. Times have changed from when a vice-chancellor's salary was, perhaps, one third more than a professor's. In Australia now, though today's professors may be paid a hundred thousand dollars and upwards, today's vice-chancellors can receive a million dollars and upwards. And in the USA, some university presidential salaries are more than two and a half million dollars! But even the USA has its problems. The football coach in one institution I know gets five times his president's salary, and perks of cars and houses! And he's worth it, judging by the amount of money gridiron brings in.

These changes may be good! But I remain to be convinced. Therefore, I am looking to you, the next generations of students, not my students (they are already retired), not my students' students (they are near retirement), but my students' students' students *(hopefully some of you, my readers)*, to understand these problems, and to have the creativity to fix them.

Furthermore, more women are being appointed in academia nowadays. **And, in the short term, this is appropriate.** But, more and more, these new appointments of women are part-time, or temporary, or terminal with little or no hope of promotion. This is not because the women are no good. It is not because older men are blocking the way. (The older men have, mostly, already disappeared. In my discipline, for instance, I was the last holder of an established professorship. There will be no more.) And the younger men are not competitors of these women; the younger men are scarcely present at all. Though better for women than before, this is still bad for women and men, both students and academics. What do you, our young people, think of all this? Are you going to enter research and teaching? Do you think such careers are for you?

And do my other readers, their parents, think that this is good for your children, whether male or female?

Of course, We (the Universities) want You, our Students
Especially we want You in all Genders and Ethnicities
BUT ARE WE GETTING YOU?

The educational ideas here are not totally new. But they are yet other ideas to be added to our current problems: fixing a pandemic, preventing climate change, producing greater social and economic equity, ridding ourselves of ethnic, religious and gender discriminations, avoiding terrorisms, wars and genocides, all in times of increasing authoritarianisms and decreasing freedoms from both the extreme left and extreme right. The single peaked 'bell' curve has long since given way to the increasingly higher 'double peak', separated by an increasingly 'deep valley'! Doing something about this has never been more important than today.

Chapter 9
Failure of Ideas: Cheating, Damned Cheating and 'Chorruption'

Have we now a choice between an old past and a new future? Can we reverse our losses in education, in questioning, learning and teaching? Can we encourage better education of the many, in society, industry and business? Can we move to a better workforce with a happier lifetime? Incentives for high skills and offers of greater security are needed. Forced disincentives must be removed, forced insecurities eliminated. All this requires making fundamental changes at every level of education: not only universities and colleges, but high schools, grade schools, kindergartens, infancy, and even in the womb.

For even the womb needs to provide positive stimulus: mothers talking, crooning, singing to the fetus; familiarity of the unborn with the other voices around: fathers, grandparents, siblings. It is well established that the child *in utero* 'recognizes' kind and happy sounds, but is 'frightened' by harsh and angry sounds. Empowering the child's mind starts in the womb. But even the womb must avoid damaging that developing mind by poverty, undernutrition, smoking, alcohol, drugs, diseases, violence (especially violence) and so on. Of course, these things actually also apply at all levels of education!

We even need to recognize the importance of the education of the smaller number of exceptional individuals who will make completely new advances. Exceptional incentives for the exceptional few will also be needed. Disincentives for them must be removed.

These things are already developing in the East, especially China. The West, especially the English-speaking West, has been doing the opposite.

In the West, we ask people to work longer by increasing retirement ages, but without providing the necessary jobs and other incentives for those longer years. We force universities to 'fire' expensive, experienced, 'permanent', older staff in favor of the 'hire' of younger, cheaper, impermanent teaching 'temps'. We generate insecurity all around! We pretend that employment has improved by counting, as employed, people who work as little as one day a week!

Education should be an 'advance guard' in the business of preparing for the complex social, economic and environmental changes that we can expect in our futures. Australia's governments (of each color, even all colors, although I am not yet sure about teal) have declared, several times, that they are strong supporters of investment in education and its infrastructure. But such declarations are denied by continual (for over nearly thirty years) cutbacks in investment in students, staff, education, infrastructure, research, development and innovation. Even the most recent attempts to push 'innovation' are little more than a partial and temporary restoration of prior savage cuts.

The best senior professors, fed up with the system, are taking redundancies. The best young research minds, with insecure low incomes, are leaving Australian academia, many even leaving Australia! How much is this resulting in increasing cheating in science and medicine (and of course also other disciplines)? And what is the resulting damage?

It leads me to ask: "Is there a difference between Cheating in academic science and medicine, Damned Cheating in scientific and medical industries, and 'Chorruption' in governmental control of science and medicine?" For none of us are whiter than white!

(With apologies to *Lies, Damned Lies and Statistics*, by Michael Wheeler, also quoted by many others including Mark Twain, but originally from Benjamin Disraeli who actually said: *Lies, Damned Lies, and **Church** Statistics.*)

Cheating

Among students, cheating is very well known; see the modern developments of the use of surrogates to take students' examinations, of the applications of computer programs like 'Turn-It-In' to 'out' cheating by students, and most recently, of artificial intelligence to produce undetectable plagiarisms!

Even among professionals, cheating, always present, has now become rampant. An early 'academic cheat' was 'The case of the Painted Butterfly' in 1702 (Figure 9.1).

Fig. 9.1. In 1702, William Charlton described a rare, one-of-a-kind, butterfly. Sixty years later the great Linnaeus declared it a new species! Thirty years after that a Danish entomologist found the specimen was a common Brimstone butterfly with painted wing spots; a ninety year 'academic cheat'.

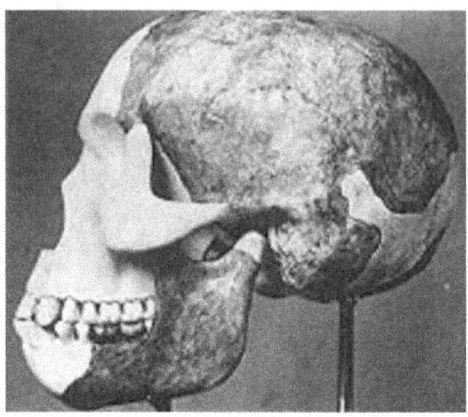

Fig. 9.2. The Piltdown fraud.

The well-known Piltdown Fraud in 1912 (Figure 9.2) also involved a 'painted' specimen (painted with photographic dichromate to make it look 'old'). This was not rooted out until 1953, a forty year 'academic cheat'!

Yet a third case was 'The Gentle Tasaday' (Figure 9.3).

The lifestyle evidence on which the book is based is shown in Figure 9.4.

And the real Tasaday people are shown in Figure 9.5.

Academic cheating has even been depicted in literature (Figure 9.6).

While the percentages of real cheatings were probably relatively stable in earlier times, they have greatly increased (by about a factor of seven) since 2000. Now the exposure times of real academic 'Cheating' are becoming shorter. Summerlin's transplantation of skin from one mouse to another ('The Case of the Painted Mouse') in 1974 was found to have been helped along by a black magic marker! Of course, this was found out within days by a technician when a swab for an injection cleaned away the blackness!

Failure of Ideas: Cheating, Damned Cheating and 'Chorruption' 193

Fig. 9.3. The title page of the book.

Fig. 9.4. The Tasaday people as displayed by the book.

Fig. 9.5. Paid to act the part.

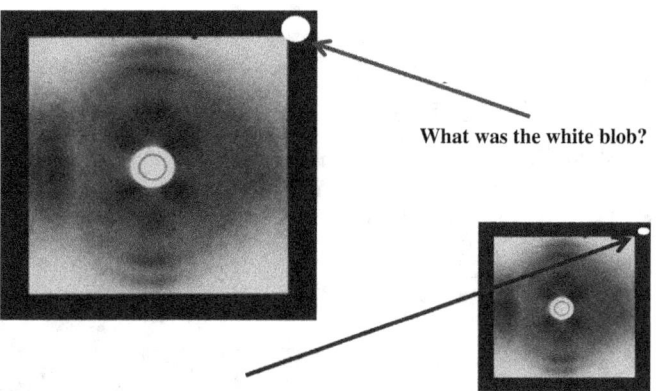

Fig. 9.6. CP Snow's fictional academic cheat in his novel *The Affair*. Of course, the enlargement of the photograph, as shown by the enlarged pinhole, changed all the measurements in his science!

Even Patients Cheat!

There is even (small-c) cheating by patients; not always cheating, sometimes a medical condition, but a problem, nevertheless.

I had my first experience of this during my student period learning psychiatry. I had to examine one patient of middle age. He was a man, of military bearing, with well-pressed trousers and black shiny shoes. He 'marched' in sharply and sat attentively. He wasn't complaining of anything. He seemed well. Nothing to start me off questioning. *Indeed, I wondered why he was there!*

Anyway, I took his clinical history which was short, his family history, which was unremarkable; and then wondered where do I go from here? Surely there had to be something wrong with him!

So, I engaged him in further conversation. What had he done? He had been in the oil industry, enjoyed it, now retired early, but quite happy. Never been married, no family. How did he get into the oil industry? Through being in North Africa during the war, was in the 8th Army with Monty and the campaign against Rommel. It was these wartime contacts that led him into the oil industry afterwards. That still didn't help me!

I asked further questions. Had he seen any action during the war? Yes, at Alexandria, and had been commended in dispatches. Anything else? Yes, in the drive towards Sicily he had been Highly Commended. Anything else? Yes, in yet further action he had received the Military Medal. Anything else? Yes, modestly and reluctantly: the Victoria Cross! Did I now have a diagnosis? Do you have a diagnosis?

By now he was quite loquacious. It eventually transpired that he had received a bar to his VC! And a few questions later still, he admitted to as many as 40 VCs! My first observation: walking with a marching or military bearing, and my last: delusions of grandeur, together, of course with later test results, indicated the complications of neurosyphilis!

I had another patient, admitted with a cough, bloody sputum, sharp localized chest pain with every small breath, among other symptoms. I thought she had pleurisy. But it took a few days in those days to get test results. In the meantime, therefore, I gave her pethidine for her pain. But by accident, I came through the curtains around her bed when she was poking the back of her throat with a small stick to cause minor bleeding. This was how she was able to (apparently) cough up blood.

I had been completely taken in. Pethidine is what she wanted! Perhaps a case of Baron von Munchausen syndrome?

A third patient (described beautifully by Lisa Sanders in *Every Patient Tells a Story*) was a young woman, hunched over the basin, vomiting, tears streaming down her face.

"I don't know if I can take this any longer! I feel like I've spent most of the last few months in hospitals and doctor's offices", she complained.

Since arriving in emergency, she had vomited continuously despite having been given several antiemetics. She was only a social smoker (pack a week), social drinker (few beers), no fevers, no cramp, no pains. Test for pregnancy, endoscopies (esophagus, stomach, colon), and possible liver, kidney and brain tests looking for causes of hyperemesis: all negative!

There was a key piece of her story missing!

One day her bed was empty! She was in the shower! Then she spoke up: she always felt better when she was in a really hot shower! I have since Googled: "persistent nausea and vomiting improved by hot showers". It gave a diagnosis I could never have guessed: cannabinoid hyperemesis.

So, you see, even patients cheat.

'Damned cheating'

A second category of cheating is by our industry, therefore 'damned cheating'. Examples here include Eric Poehlman,

Malcolm Pearce, Hwang Woo-Suk, and especially Andrew Wakefield, all physicians in top institutions!

Poehlman, doing research into aging, menopause and hormones, pleaded guilty to falsifying seventeen grant applications and inventing data in ten research papers! He was the first scientist jailed for scientific fraud: 'damned cheating'.

Pearce, an obstetrician, reported transplantation of an ectopic uterus with live birth! But he did this by hacking computers to alter notes, and inventing patients in a study of polycystic ovary syndrome.

Hwang Woo-Suk reported landmark work in *Science*, but with data that were falsified and fabricated. He even used unethical means requiring female staff members to superovulate!

Yet again, notwithstanding being found out, and even being retracted, some such cheatings can persist for many years. Thus, a 'many years' example is that of Andrew Wakefield who linked autism with the MMR vaccine. This, in spite of several retractions, is still 'evidence' used by the anti-vaccination lobby!

Perhaps damned cheating has always existed, but Figure 9.7 implies it is worse now.

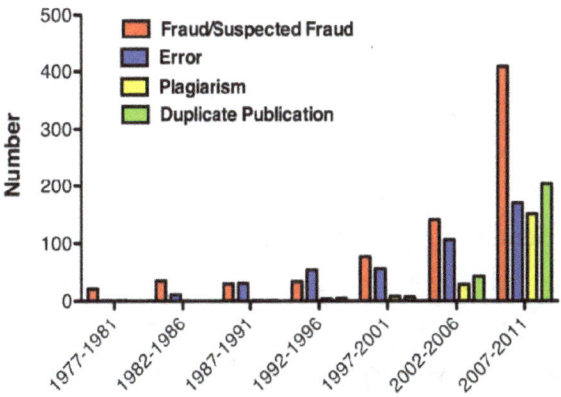

Fig. 9.7. Some statistics on damned cheating.

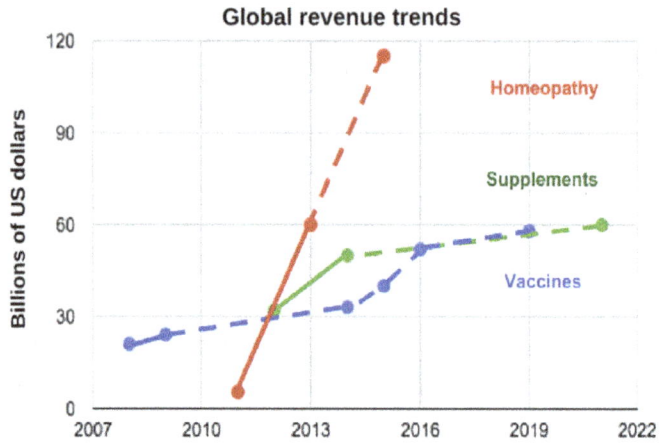

Fig. 9.8. Following the money: statistics for some treatments.

'Damned Cheating' is also undertaken by medical industries. Martin Shkreli, age 32, marked up a 5,000 percent increase in the price of Daraprim. He was also convicted in a $US 11 million embezzlement probe at another of his companies: Retrophin.

Again, whenever one has an allergic reaction due to insect bites, the effective medicine for it is epinephrine. Mylan Pharma developed an auto-injector called EpiPen which helps in injecting epinephrine. And they jacked up the price by 400 percent! Figure 9.8 is of interest here.

But the Worst Kind of Cheating is 'Chorruption'

'Chorruption', to coin a word, is cheating about science and medicine by politicians and governments.

For example, Edward Levi (president of the University of Chicago during my time there in the 1960s, and a very distinguished lawyer) served for a period as Attorney General of the United States. In 1976, he wrote a memo to President Gerald Ford in which he said "the 'loss' of radioactive substances from a government facility should be investigated further". In particular he wrote that: if there was even a possibility that government officials "may have participated in or concealed an offence, it would be necessary to conduct an investigation".

This matter involved the disappearance of powerful radioactive materials, great enough and potent enough to produce bombs, to arm nations, to start wars. It may rank, perhaps, as one of the most serious of government 'Chorruptions' of that time; and it could have had most serious ultimate effects on people and peace.

Edward's investigation was never followed up by government! And I only heard about the matter in 2015, though others knew about it earlier!

As the eminent jurist Sir William Blackstone commented centuries ago:

> *"The body of the charter has unfortunately been gnawn (sic) by rats."*
> *"We must not let our fears, our alienation, our selfishness, our xenophobia, or our smugness allow our leaders to take up the task that the rats left unfinished."*

'Chorruption', then, is not just a creature of recent governmental problems (such as the global financial meltdown of 2008, or the Covid pandemic of 2020). Its history can be documented over many years by the history of what happened to advice on science (and medicine, technology, engineering, and mathematics) to governments. I have my own personal experiences of this.

Advice on Science to Governments in the UK in my 'Earlier Years'

As the last full-time student of anatomist Professor Solly Zuckerman, I was much aware of the other part of his life, advising government on war, defense and science.

Zuckerman was involved in the science of the war effort (1939–1945), and later in giving classified advice on science and defense (1945–1960). He then became chief science advisor to the prime minister and the government (1960–1971). After retirement, he continued to serve as consultant on science to the government. And he continued to serve as a peer in the House of Lords until his death in 1993, with many contributions in Hansard and on government committees. One of his books (1982) was entitled *Nuclear Illusion and Reality* (Figure 9.9).

In all this career, he served both Labor and Conservative governments, and for much of this time had a direct line to the prime ministers of the day (of both political colors!), a lifetime's service in science to government.

Fig. 9.9. Zuckerman's book cover.

Contrast this with what followed. The next two science advisers served for 2–3 years to single prime ministers. The next three served for three years each, but only as cabinet undersecretaries. The final four served with no direct links to prime ministers at all. Further, most served only during the tenures of single political parties. Few served government in any major way after their terminations.

Talking up science by politicians, but reducing its influence on governments and especially on prime ministers, has been a long-term policy in the UK, and it still goes on.

A Small Window on Science Advice in the USA from my 'Middle Years'

Wars always seem so 'good' for science!

During and after the Second World War, major US influences on science (and technology, engineering, and mathematics) continued due to individuals like Vannevar Bush (the overseer of the Manhattan Project), Philip Handler (designer of the National Science Foundation), and George Marshall (creator of the Marshall Plan). These followed the major wartime science foci of Roosevelt and Truman, and were continued into the immediate postwar period by Eisenhower.

Then came the total abandonment of science and technology advice by Nixon! Maybe this was the beginning of the science downfall in the USA!

However, my personal knowledge of what was going on in the USA related to my 'middle years' (in the 1970s and 80s). Thus, as graduate dean at the University of Southern California, I served alongside the college dean, Jack Marburger. Marburger was a top physicist and academic administrator at USC; he later became president of Stony Brook, the jewel in the crown of the State University of New York; later still, director of the Brookhaven National Laboratory, and finally science advisor to the first President Bush.

In this last position Marburger ran into difficulties. His office was originally next to the President in the White House, with the ability to walk in on the President at any time! Later, he was removed to the opposite end of the White House away from the President! Finally, he was located in a separate building far down Pennsylvania Avenue!

With these office banishments went reductions in reporting lines. He originally reported directly to the President. Later he reported to the President only through the White House media apparatus! Then the media office started to shorten his reports, even modifying them without reference back to him, even deleting information! Finally, the media office totally subverted his reports, providing the President with different data and advice!

I have no personal information about what followed in the USA as I then moved to Australia, though, of course, I am especially aware of Donald Trump's banning of the use of words like abortion, pregnancy, contraceptives, experiments, testing, etc. by White House officials.

My 'Johnny-come-lately' Knowledge of Scientific Advice in Australia

What happened in Australia? This, of course, is a story from my 'elder years', 1987 and onwards, and is merely observation! I was never in it!

The first two chief scientists of Australia were appointed for two to three years respectively, and were full time. The first advised the prime minister, but the second only advised the cabinet.

The next three were also appointed for short periods, two to four years, but were only part time, (one worked as little as one day per week!). A fourth resigned in two years! A fifth held the position for five years, but then retired. The current advisor has been in harness only a short time. Until Covid19, none of these excellent individuals had a direct line to the prime minister.

One of our chief scientists (Ian Chubb, author of the *Health of Australian Science* report) said, optimistically, of science: "We do not have a train wreck".

But he also said Australia is: "The only OECD country without a science or technology strategy". And he hoped (was it wishful thinking?) that: "Australia in 2025 will be strong, prosperous, healthy, secure, and positioned to benefit all Australians in a rapidly changing world".

I wonder!

The problem is that, like Prime Minister Margaret Thatcher (herself previously a scientist) in the UK, like Presidents Bush and Trump in the USA, recent Australian prime ministers such as Tony Abbott and Scott Morrison did not really want to follow the science, probably did not even believe the science.

Subverting Science Advice and Scientific Advisors

These changes in my three countries are having not unexpected effects. There is a suppression of accounts, analyses and advices that diverge from preferred political policies. There is injection of political desires into scientific and medical determinations. There is the effect of many other groups (ideological politicians, self-interested industrialists, even religious representatives) interfering with overall scientific (STEM) advice.

These interferences are achieved by many mechanisms, not the least of which are the stacking of scientific advisory panels, and the examining of the same questions sequentially until the advice that is wanted is obtained! How many reports on taxation, on education, on health, on the aged, on the disabled, on poverty, on inequity, on various discriminations, on climate, (on many of the country's other problems), have been commissioned by how many governments in Australia? And what mice have been delivered from such pregnant elephants?

These interferences are carried out by limiting askable questions, by constraining the methods that can be used to seek answers, by restricting the selection of who provides advice, by suppressing findings in conflict with government policies, by sanctioning misleading claims to bolster 'approved' results, and by placing ideologically 'approved' people in charge.

All this has had a chilling effect on science and scientists. Retribution is exacted against those who ask unapproved questions, or produce unwanted results. This pressure can even stem from the universities themselves, as administrators remove the academic freedom to criticize. Some specific scientific examples include: stem cell research, condoms and HIV, abortion, cancer, prostate imaging, and, of course, global warming.

Furthermore, this governmental cheating may be very serious and long term. It is often concealed by such phrases as 'Not in the Public Interest', 'Sequestered for Fifty Years' and 'Freedom of Information' (which is designed, in Australia, as in the USA, to keep information secret). And how much is Figure 9.10 a part of the problem?

Fig. 9.10. What a great picture for another book cover!

To put it bluntly (and alliteratively): this is 'Chorruption'!

Of course, we should all be doing something about this. Particularly when I retired, this would have been a good time for me to have participated. But in retirement I have had so much exciting science that I never took up the challenge.

The Activist Challenge

So, it has only been at this very late stage in my life (almost as I am retiring from retirement) that I have started to look more seriously at these kinds of problems. It stems, in part, from work over many years helping Pan Ruliang and many other Chinese colleagues. Thus, I was appointed, in 2022, Honorary Executive Committee Member of the Board of the International Biodiversity and Primate Conservation Centre (IBPCC), housed at Dali University, Yunnan Province. It operates through Dali and Northwest Universities (in this latter of which I have been an honorary visiting professor).

This center aims to share the combined experience and expertise of international experts in conservation biology, genetics, behavior, ecology, disease, ecosystem health and environmental sustainability. The aim is to work with regional and national scientists, conservation organizations, governmental officials, the media, educators and the public, to help preserve, protect, and restore natural habitats and environments of threatened plants, animals and humans.

All this has led me to a small attempt (next chapter) to correct what I should have been doing in retirement: attempting to provide my ideas into the above, and other even broader problems.

Chapter 10
My Mistakes: Ideas I Missed!

All these ideas about: teaching and research, science and medicine, education and academia, how universities work, how they are controlled, and most of all about individuals: students, teachers, researchers and administrators have 'festered' in my mind for many years.

Teaching and Research: Past and Present

My first teaching was with two equally young colleagues in Solly Zuckerman's department in the University of Birmingham, UK. All three of us decided that our teaching should not be the fixed memorization of facts, but the changing understanding of ideas.

> *"In science, one must search for ideas. If there are no ideas, then there is no science.*
> *Facts without ideas clutter up the mind and the memory".*
> *(Belinskii [1811–1848], reported 1948).*

Our new teaching offerings were never questioned, never even 'questionnaired', and certainly never 'bureaucratized'. We were just *trusted* to get on with the job! We *gloried* in our students' excellent results. We worked so *enthusiastically* for them. They worked *incredibly hard* for us. Many lifelong friendships and top careers resulted!

A similar thing happened in research in that department. We were thrown in at the deep end. Lifelines were available; but the research atmosphere was so exciting, there was so much discussion among us all, that lifelines were rarely needed.

> "It is important that we bring a certain ragamuffin, barefoot irreverence to our studies.
> We are not here to worship what is known, but to question it."
> (modified from Bronowski, 1975).

Coffee time was a time for swapping science. And because of the mores of that department, very exciting science indeed!

> "To live for a time close to great minds is the very best form of education."
> (John Buchan, 1940).

Educating had not degenerated into what it is now, grumbles about impossible administrative and teaching loads, little or no funding, few or no jobs, major job insecurity, and loss of the best minds!

Collegiality and the Academy

In effect, then, in those days, in both teaching and research, we felt bonded to each other, to the exciting minds with whom we conversed, to the living department in which we were located, to the medical school as a whole, and even to the university: old-fashioned ideas.

Though we were, of course, *just employees*', we felt that we were more than just employees. We felt we had stakes in our students, our colleagues, our disciplines, and our institutions that were so much greater than those of 'mere' employees: more old-fashioned ideas!

Years later (in the 1960s), an initiative at the University of Chicago was to give me such feelings in spades! The Board of Trustees (somewhat equivalent to an Australian university senate) decided it would start a major fundraising campaign. In those days, this was new. But the board decided it would only do it if it could be shown, before going public, that the academic staff supported the idea of the campaign.

The result: the academic staff (about a thousand at that time) raised preliminary money for the fund: to an average of $1,000 per individual (at a time when salaries were a small fraction of what they are now)! Eleanor and I, both new and young, together gave that average amount. Can you imagine Australian university staff today being motivated to give to their university like that?

It was to be very many years later still, that such old-fashioned ideas were to be gradually lost, that 'students' would become an amorphous cloud of 'clients', hidden behind computer screens, and that 'academics' would gradually become 'just employees', in thrall to 'employers', even to 'owners'.

The 'collegial academy', dedicated to teaching, learning and discovery, would be gradually closed down and replaced by a 'business house', with a 'commercial ethos', run by 'managers' for 'clients'. The managers would decide what we should do, how we should be judged, *and when we should be terminated*! And the managers themselves were not 'in charge'. They, in their turn, were in thrall to government.

The Academy after Retirement

Thus, when eventually I retired, I thought that I ought to contribute to discussions about these changes. After all, I thought I knew quite a lot about universities, from three professorships, three deanships, across three continents, and over three vicennia!

My experiences included ideas about teaching and learning in our discipline, about extending it downwards into the high schools, widening it into the general undergraduate curriculum, and upwards into postgraduate levels. It further included interactions with the retired and the indigenous.

It emphasized the importance of interacting with the best minds, the leavening of solitary research by collaboration, the moving from within a single discipline to the intersections between disciplines, the extending of standard conventional thinking to new imaginative thinking, and the 'borrowing' of ideas and technologies from other disciplines, even from industry and, paradoxically, from components of government. (For instance, I had had contacts with Britain's Agricultural Research Council, the Isle of Wight's Westland's Aircraft, the UK government's Home Office, with the USA's Bell Telephone Labs (as it was called then), the Kansas State Geological Survey, and with Australia's CSIRO and CSL, among other organizations.) In other words, my academic life seemed to have prepared me for these wider challenges.

However, I quickly found, on retirement in 1997, that my own academic work was to enter a new phase. My research funding was, luckily, and surprisingly, to continue for a further two decades. I was to enjoy new international collaborations. My teaching was to be what I wanted to offer. And I was no longer constrained by administration!

Thus, in retirement, I have done more research, published more papers and books, obtained more grants, and had more graduate students and colleagues, even had new interactions with interested retirees, than, perhaps, at any other comparable time in my life. *If I could, why wouldn't I?*

But also, as a result, I had no time for that wider challenge, until this book. Yet the challenge remains.

The Academy in the West

The universities of the West are usually described as getting better and better, but are actually becoming worse and worse. They are increasingly being overtaken by some of the universities of the East.

Almost everywhere in the West there are fewer teachers but more teaching, more administrators yet more administration required of teachers, and less research by even fewer researchers. Most are required to do more with less!

In Australia, the effect has been especially pernicious. By every measure of science and mathematics, of industrial research engagement, of patents and commercialization, of intellectual property, and of the ability to seize on all these things, Australia is not a leading nation. Indeed, it is in decline. Public funding for education (in constant dollars) is about one third of what it was when I first came here thirty-five years ago! In such statistics, we are now (as of 2019) last but one in the OECD.

In the light of this continued research and teaching decline, and because the changed institutional background seems to be such an unmitigated and continuing disaster, I felt I could not make a dent in the tsunami. I did not take up the challenge. I continued my research and teaching. I enjoyed it. I probably saved myself a lot of heartache.

But perhaps I should have spoken up. Perhaps I should have thrown myself on the pyre. The smoke might just have been white!

The Academy in the East

Things have been different in many of the countries of the East. Because of the accidents of my research travels and collaborations, I have some special knowledge here. Most Asian universities have been zooming upwards! Of course, it is true that many of them generally started from a much lower base. That made it easier to climb.

China, in particular, was at absolute ground zero as a result of its Cultural Revolution, when universities were closed, and staff, especially older professors, were sent to the fields where many of them died. However, from a base at the University of Hong Kong, I was in China several times in the years following.

In this phase, China started tackling **the idea of getting the teaching going**. It was wonderful how quickly it all happened. On my first visit to mainland China (1980), I visited new one-year 'barefoot doctor' medical schools. There were two-year medical schools on my second visit two years later. And four-year medical schools only a few years after that. Incredible growth! Impossible in the West!

China also knew that that communicating knowledge (teaching) without also adding to knowledge (research) is sterile. So, China tackled **the idea of getting the research going**.

Thus, on my first visit, my Chinese hosts had wanted me to talk about the uses of computers in biology, especially in human structure and development. But of course, they had no computers! Two years later (the meetings started on a two-year basis) local Chinese colleagues gave two papers using computers; not very good papers, but at least they were doing it. Two years later, there was a little session on the use of computers (of course, still only desktops!). Today, China has the best supercomputers in the world, better than the US. Fantastic change, unmatched in the West! Of course, the nature of government in China is such that all this was mandated!

Also, at that time, I was asked to discuss with Chinese colleagues what research in human development (one of their particular interests) they might do. As a result, I became aware that they had hundreds of human specimens in museum pots at different stages of 'pre-natal' development: at three months, four months, five months ... at seven months, eight months, nine months ... at eleven months (!), twelve months (!), thirteen months (!)'. This was the result of course, not just of natural losses, but of embryocides, feticides, and infanticides!

Most of these specimens seemed normal, the result of the application of the 'one-child policy'! Of course, at that point I knew nothing about that policy. When I got back to the USA, I wondered about it! Should I talk to the US State Department? Should I talk to anybody? And then I came to my senses. I was not the only visitor in China. Far more senior Americans had been there before me. It was obvious the US government knew all about this but was keeping quiet! So, I said nothing and I'm sorry; though I doubt it would have done any good.

But I did do some other things to help my Chinese hosts. Through Professor Peter Lisowski, University of Hong Kong, I arranged to have many, unwanted in Australia, second-hand textbooks shipped to them.

And they asked: "Will you please read anatomical terms into a tape recorder? We don't know how to pronounce the words." So, there may well be a generation of doctors in China who pronounce anatomical terms with a 'North Country English' accent. (The word 'malleolus' is pronounced 'mal-Ã-uh-lus' in Oxford and Cambridge, but 'mally-Oh-LUs' in the English North Country.)

I was even asked to help them write CVs. They were all so keen to go abroad for further education. "What is this thing called a CV?", they asked. "We don't have them." So, I quizzed them. "You teach?", they agreed. "You have written materials about your teaching, they are the equivalent of a CV teaching portfolio." "You do research", they agreed. "You have no journals (at that time) but you write research reports; they are the equivalent of CV publications." And so, I helped them to prepare CVs to go abroad.

On one of these visits to China, at breakfast, we invited two Chinese colleagues to dine with us while we discussed what we might do to help. All went well until it came time to pay — of course, we expected to pay for our Chinese colleagues. But the hotel wanted our Chinese colleagues to pay for themselves, about ten times as much, dining in the foreign guests' dining room than they would have paid in their own dining room. We were not supposed to know about the differential, and we certainly did not want our guests to pay so much more. The matter nearly caused an international incident. Luckily, the president of the Chinese Association was high up in the party, so the whole thing was settled quietly.

At another time, I attended an official dinner for the foreign guests. After several speeches by Chinese hosts, it became apparent that the foreign guests would have to respond. There were only four of us. Two of our company were relatively young and did not really want to speak *al fresco* in public. Peter Lisowski was much older but he also did not like making speeches. It was clearly going to rest on me. I wondered what to say.

Having had to wait in Guangzhou Airport for an hour, I had noticed that, on a very high white wall, there was painted a poem by Mao Tse-tung, of course, in Chinese characters. But next to it was painted an English translation. I was so taken by the translation that I spent twenty minutes reading and memorizing it. I decided to recite it in my talk in a dramatic way.

I spoke thus:

> "The Red Army ... fears not ... the trials ... of the long march.
> To them ... a thousand hills ... ten thousand rivers ... are nothing".

I had wondered if it was appropriate to recite this poem because I thought Mao was out of favor at that time. But the poem was still on the wall so I thought it must be alright.

I had no sooner uttered the first line, then it was clear that the entire audience, English and non-English speakers talking together, knew what I was saying, and were delighted. I could not have chosen a better offering.

Later over drinks, one Chinese colleague, I seem to remember it was Ju Gong, from Xian, (his daughter, Ju Li, works with us now at UWA), asked me why I recited the poem with a changed dramatic voice, and with gaps around phrases. "Oh," I said, "it seemed such a martial poem that I recited it the way I thought Churchill would have done, even mimicking Churchill's voice and idiom!"

There were so many beautiful metaphors. At one point in the poem, I used the words:

> "The river rolled by in muddy spate".

Why did I say that, Ju Gong wanted to know? I explained that when my local river, the river Weir, in England, was running fast and swollen after a storm, the earth on the river bed would be stirred into ripples of mud. I thought that was the metaphor Mao was using for the marching of the soldiers.

Ju Gong laughed. "No," he said, "the words were referring to the way the potter rolls pellets of clay by throwing them along the ground, to make them round." But it was indeed a metaphor: for the army marching quickly onward.

I also loved the final phrases:

"Warm are the cliffs by the waters of golden sand,
Cold are the iron chains that bind the waters of Tatu.
The Three Armies march on; each face is glowing."

That was a most successful after-dinner talk!

Even earlier, China had realized the importance of support for science and universities.

"We must catch up with this advanced level of world science ...
either in peaceful competition **... or in any aggressive war ...** *which the enemy may unleash."*
(Chou En-lai, Report on the Question of the Intellectuals, 1956.)

I was also involved in those days in discussions about a new medical school for the (then) new Chinese University (at Shatin) with its first vice-chancellor, M. C. Lee. He dearly wanted an 'American' medical school, and of course, I had knowledge of both UK and US systems. And I also had discussions with the next vice-chancellor, Ma Lin, whom I had first met at a Macy Foundation Conference in the USA.

But it was not to be. The General Medical Council (Britain) wanted a traditional British medical school. And that is what the new Chinese University got!

As in the new China, new support of teaching and research also occurred in India, Indonesia, Singapore, South Korea, Thailand, Vietnam and many other Asian countries. All are pouring money into universities, science, medicine, research **and their academics** as if there were no tomorrow.

Of course, these countries have an advantage that we of the West do not have.

They all respect, even revere: age, thinking, wisdom, teaching, learning, and the individuals involved in them.

Western customs: the generally negative views of education, the low status of teachers and academics, especially of older ones, much enmity towards new thinking and new ideas, all militate so strongly against academia.

In fact, in Australia, the very word 'academic' is often pejorative!

"Bail Out Universities Rather than Banks?"

We, in the West, are continually ordering 'independent bodies' to examine our problems. Not one, but many, reports have been written: on taxation, immigration, unemployment, health services, disability benefits, retirement pensions, social inequities, immigration policies, and goodness knows what else. Most such reports aim to close the gap between the 'haves' and 'have-nots'. But the policies that follow, contrary-wise, serve to increase those gaps. They cause further damage to the poor, the old, the sick, the disabled, the unemployed (especially the unemployed young and the unemployed old), the female (in many ways), the immigrant, and the destitute.

In many countries, today, attempts to fix these serious problems are being countered by *increasing misinformation*, especially using the *language of demonization*. It is a strategy of the far right, and in a different way, sometimes also a strategy of the far left, with increasing separations between these factions. For example, Australia's right does not believe in global warming, and refuses to help the center deal with the problem. Equally, however, Australia's far left, wanting to deal with global warming, refuses to take the smaller steps towards it that are offered by the middle ground.

Further, these contrary strategies are signaling abandonment of the idea that everyone should be equal before the law.

So has it been with bodies examining education, especially university education. Report follows report. Commission follows commission. All point to problems. All suggest improvement. The results seem always to be the opposite. Education is further damaged; quality further falls; usually the teachers are blamed!

This is not a new phenomenon in the West. I have never forgotten Harold Wilson's (one time UK Labour Prime Minister) 1960s speech about "The white-hot fires of technology"! Within a week of that speech, English house sales plummeted; luckily, we had just sold ours prior to emigration to the USA. Almost immediately also, the pound dived in relation to the US dollar; again, luckily, in preparation for our move, we had already exchanged our pounds for dollars. The very act of talking about the "white-hot fires of technology" meant that they were to be largely snuffed out! This seems also to apply to today's calls for 'science innovation' in Australia.

Is it not time to recognize that education is a key to national improvement, not a drain on the public purse? Removing money from education does not help the economy! The economy is helped by pumping money into education, into universities, into colleges and into schools, even down to kindergartens and childcare.

Yet it is useless to pump money into just one part of such an integrated system. A system that 'flows' must flow in all parts!

Should we not, therefore, support education as much as economics, banks, deficits and currencies? Is not this important for our nation, indeed, possibly, all nations?

The Rise and Fall of Nations

It turns out that a distinguished economist, Ray Dalio, has recently spoken to the past, present and future of nations. He has defined what he considers to be the principal factors that have raised some nations up and pushed some down, in both the short and long terms. The first two of these factors he identifies are obvious: **Economics** and **Disorder**.

Dalio's economic factors comprise, for example, not only economic principles but their related measures: population size, life expectancy, mortality from disease and malnutrition, and gender and age structure. One obvious economic measure is the burden of debt.

On such economic factors, the data for the USA, although obviously still in first place, **has been reducing for at least two decades**. In total contrast, China, during that same time, from starting close to the bottom (an 'underdeveloped' country) **is by far the most improved**. From being almost at the bottom, it is now second, below the USA (but see below).

Dalio's disorder factors depend upon the idea that, when acting in cooperation and avoiding wasting resources on arguing, fighting and corruption, nations (and the individuals within them) can rise markedly. However, when nations are disordered, without cooperation, with corruptions, antagonisms, even fighting, even hating, then they waste resources (and even lives). How do today's nations appear on a disorder scale?

On a disorder scale, comprising the fighting between the far right and almost everyone else, the USA **is now poorer** than any other first-world country. Though this has been powerfully obvious for some six years now, it has actually been operating for many decades.

Eleanor and I did not realize this when we moved to the United States. It was especially hidden from us at first because we worked in a very high-quality university (The University of Chicago) and lived in a high-level multiracial area (Hyde Park). The disorder between many elements of the right and left in the USA, although always present, was much less evident to a British newcomer in such a milieu.

However, since then, the disorder factor in the USA, actually at that time already quite bad, has become very much worse. The latest damages (worst of all in Trump times), are caused by (in no particular order): the gun lobby, the anti-abortion push, the anti-immigration stance, the many varieties of racial barriers, the sex and gender fights, the religious antagonisms, the continued activities of the Ku Klux Klan and Nazi organizations, and many disinformation and denier groups.

China also has major **internal** disorder factors. But, in contrast, many of these tend to be hidden: such as the Tiananmen Square matter, the camps for 're-education' of Uighurs, the imprisonment of top industrialists, the high-rise property recession, the police state changes in Hong Kong, even Covid factors and statistics, and so on. There are powerful attempts to conceal them. All this is because concealment can be, and is, centrally mandated.

And there are also new levels of disorder for China that are **external**: China's attentions to the Pacific Islands, South China Sea, South Korea, South Vietnam, Singapore, Australia, and others.

(Taiwan is an interesting question that, for China, is both external and internal.) China's external attentions even extend to Europe, the Middle East, Africa and South America, via the snares of its Belt and Road initiatives and its playing of the authoritarian game.

But in the longer term, China's all-powerful president, and the autocratic Chinese Communist Party (CCP), may be unable to hold down international reactions to these. China's threat to Taiwan, its support of Russia in the Ukraine, its aggressions in the South China Sea, and more widely in the Indo-Pacific region, and its unacceptable uses of commercial pressure, espionage, cyber-warfare, and interference in the politics of other nations, seem unlikely to go away. The harder China pushes these things, the more most other countries are pushing back, thus resulting in the formation of new international alliances and the strengthening of old antagonisms. But it is at least possible that China is starting to realize these effects, and may be coming to adopt a reciprocal commitment to at least a somewhat peaceful coexistence.

Dalio's Unusual Education Factor

Economics and disorder, as described above, are obvious. However, the surprising third factor that Dalio recognizes as incredibly important is his **education factor** (based upon science, engineering, technology, mathematics, and their applications and innovations). **This factor, Dalio also shows, has a major effect on the futures of nations.** (Of course, he recognizes that his major factors are not totally separate and are inevitably linked.) But let us examine what he found in this surprising third factor.

In the **education factor**, though the USA still stood first of all nations (as of 2017), that measure has, in fact, been slowly falling for more than 30 years. The degree of this had been somewhat hidden because most other Western nations were also declining in that same time.

In that same period, and in marked contrast, the **education factor** for China has risen. From being almost nowhere 40 years ago, it stood (by 2018) a close second to the USA.

And there is every likelihood that, by the end of this year (2023), China will stand first. And because not all is known about a secretive China, following former leader Deng Xiaoping's mantra:

"Hide your strength, bide your time",

it is possible that China may be already higher and stronger than anyone outside knows.

(Australia is ranked almost lowest [eighteenth] of the OECD countries!)

This **education factor** is a complex based on **all the basic and applied sciences**: physics, chemistry, biology, mathematics, engineering, technology, social, psychological and medical, but particularly applications of computers (including AI and other thinking technologies). It applies to many domains of human activity, especially to improving productivity and living standards. Computers, in contrast to humans, have far more memory, are much more accessible, work incredibly more quickly, and avoid emotional mistakes (though they can make serious implanted errors, and are markedly prone to hacking, to being hacked, and to autocratic control).

The particular collaboration between humans and computers is capable of producing radical improvements in almost every area of life. My own heart is not only a creature of my living pacemaker (which is not so good), but also a creature of my electronic pacemaker. It can be monitored and has even been altered, through the cloud, with no hands on!

There are many further possibilities on the horizon. They could have enormous economic and related effects upon humanity, as scientific advances lead to almost unimaginable changes in global wealth and power. Perhaps almost equally, however, they can lead to almost unimaginable advances in rates of learning, providing humans with vastly greater powers to see the present and to understand, and perhaps, partially shape the future.

This **education factor** should allow the quality of human life to increase over the next decades, not only for many obvious reasons, but also for some that we cannot visualize at present. A few such already on the horizon are: AI and robotics in health care, health monitoring and advice-providing wearables, advances in the practical uses of changing genes and genomes, molecular improvements in vaccines for viral diseases, cancers, and heritable disorders, and breakthroughs in many nutritional and pharmaceutical treatments. It is even likely that there will be changes that only a science fiction addict could guess (but not predict).

However, the **education factor** also depends upon interactions with the economic and disorder factors. While these have changed but little in China, in the USA they have further impacted negatively on education.

Future Prospects for all Nations Depend Upon these Key Factors

Thus, the United States was clearly the top power twenty years ago in all three factors. But recent years have seen the overall position of the USA weaken. Though partly due to **worsening in the economic and internal disorder factors**, Dalio shows that it is also, and perhaps surprisingly, due to **marked worsening in the**

education factor. These downward movements together mean that, for some years now, from being very high, the USA has been in gradual decline, and is now in increasingly greater decline.

In contrast, China, ranked very poorly thirty years ago, has now risen to second position overall. And because of our lack of knowledge about the **hidden factors**, China may, indeed, already be first. This improvement, Dalio shows, is based not only on raised **economic factors** and hidden **disorder factors**, but also, quite oppositely, on an unexpected great rise in the **education factors**.

Thus, with all this as background, the new, third, absolute contrast between China and the USA, is the **education factor**. Not previously recognized as very important, it now looms large, but in opposite directions for the two countries. It is markedly up for China (and some other Asian nations), but strongly down for the USA (and the West in general).

Yet everything is not well for China. In more recent years, China has been showing rumbles of problems in **economic factors**, and of major dissent in the **disorder factors**. Thus, though China's overall position may still seem to be improving, it may actually be weakening due to autocratic efforts to control economics and to hide disorder. Despite the rise in China's **education factors,** China's overall position may already have turned negative, and this may fall ever more quickly.

The interactions between nations are also important. Thus, **China's inward-looking mindset** is being further entrenched by the United States, which has stepped up technology wars with China. **America's isolated mindset** (earlier less evident when helping post-Second-World-War Europe and Asia) has now coincided with China's arrival on the global market, and its growing influence since the early 2000s.

The position of China is further affected by more recent pressures being brought to bear on its smaller neighbors: Macao, Hong Kong, Taiwan, North Korea, Laos, Cambodia, and possibly increasingly on Japan, Singapore, South Korea, Pacific Island Nations, Australia, and, not impossibly, yet other Asian countries. This is starting to lead to an increased US interest in Asia.

Nowhere has the combination of Xi Jinping's assertive foreign policies and Trump's American withdrawals had greater impacts than in Asia's backyard.

As Beijing's powers have grown, so has Washington's unease. As a result, after years of see-sawing, the many countries in the west, especially the USA, are trying to re-engage with non-Chinese Asia.

Making my own small contribution to the problems of our education factor, even if it would have been just publicizing a grumble, is what I did not do in retirement. I, therefore, lost 25 years! It is my hope that you, who come after, will avoid my mistakes and lost years.

Of course, We (the Universities) want You, our Students
Especially we want You in all Genders and Ethnicities.
And we say we want you in STEM: Science, Technology, Engineering and Mathematics.
But while STEM is good: S(S)TE(AH)M(M) is better!
The bracketed parts of this new, if awkward, acronym, (S)(AH)(M), stand for the generally forgotten, but also creative, parts of learning: Sociology, Arts, Humanities, and Medicine.
We, in the West, seem to have largely given up on them!
Do you understand? Are you going to join my diatribe?
A caveat and a thank you

It is almost impossible to explain how fantastically I have enjoyed my academic journey, its stimuli and ideas. And how wonderful to be able to share them with many students, of all ages. (Amazingly, I have given lectures, just this year, where I was by no means the oldest person in the room!)

Though at first a doctor who treated patients, then a lecturer who taught students, eventually I became a professor, *questioning* theories (researching), *exciting* students (teaching), and *challenging* how it all works. 'Challenging' is the most important word. We are not here to worship ideas, but to challenge them.

As a member of the 'Silent Generation' (born in the period 1925–1945), like my peers, I accepted authority and did not challenge it. I now break that 'silence' to speak to you: fellow students of more recent generations, especially Z and Alpha (1997–2025).

Your careers will, eventually, be very different from mine. Unlike my generation, your generations have better personal technologies, span greater ethnic diversities, accept more mixed identities, understand more diverse family dynamics, and will undergo many more changes in a much more accelerating world, than ever I did. But it also looks as though you will have much greater difficulties in having yourselves accepted.

For again, in contrast to me, you face greater economic inequalities, than I ever did. My whole education, from infant playgroup through doctorate in science, was free — I had no debts. Further, and also in contrast to me, you have far greater worries about personal bullying, ethnic divisiveness, media misinformation, increased governmental authoritarianism, unchecked, indeed worsening, climate crises, much more polluted environments, old and new pandemics, and recrudescences of old wars and rumors of new.

I come out of my silence, out of my failure to protest, to encourage you, even to urge you, the newer generations, to challenge what I, as a teacher, researcher, practitioner, organizer and even just a concerned citizen, failed to do. I want my past failures to show you the way to your successes.

I must also record that this book is based not only on almost illegible handwritten diary pages, but also upon unreadable paper tapes, crumpled IBM cards, old computer outputs, out-of-date audio cassettes, varieties of USB sticks and video discs, even losses in the cloud, but most of all upon memories, often somewhat faded, and sometimes, too, partially incorrect.

So, not everything I have written here is true. Though I have notes, many are almost indecipherable; though I have memories, many of them are fading fast; though I have colleagues who could help, many are now gone! In fact, I am now the last student alive from my particular student cohort!

But I have a loyal wife, a librarian in a previous life. Her librarian's 'organizationship' has brought order to the whole thing, and has reduced my accidental 'cheating' to just my slovenly 'checking'!

I hope you will find these ideas, though curious, unusual, even heretical, as at least stimulating, and as exciting to you as they have been to me. But I also hope that you, in your turn, will challenge them, find them wrong, and will, in turn, be stimulated to produce yet better ideas. These will, in further turn, excite those coming after you, help them to test your new ideas, and find them wrong! This is the essence of education.

Charles Oxnard
Professor Emeritus and Senior Honorary Research Fellow,
School of Human Sciences and College of Emeriti,
University of Western Australia

Books by the author

The Musculature of the Primate Shoulder

Form and Pattern in Human Evolution: Some Mathematical, Physical and Engineering Approaches

Primate Locomotion: Some Links with Evolution and Morphology

Uniqueness and Diversity in Human Evolution: Morphometric Studies of Australopithecines

The Order of Man: A Biomathematical Anatomy of the Primates

Animal Lifestyles and Anatomies: The Case of the Prosimian Primates

Fossils, Teeth and Sex: New Perspectives on Human Evolution

Human Adaptability: Future Trends and Lessons from the Past

Endemic Cretinism

Ghostly Muscles, Wrinkled Brains, Heresies and Hobbits

Anatomical Terms and their Derivation

The Scientific Bases of Human Anatomy

Aiming at Medicine: A Human Biology, Health Sciences and Medical Career Approach

Change and Challenge in Human Structure — Sixty Years On

Chapter 11
An Eighth Idea out of the Ordinary: Damages to Learning!

The work of Dalio, cited in Chapter 10, demonstrates how the rise and fall of nations, though obviously measured by Economy and Disorder, are also, perhaps rather surprisingly, related to Education, to Learning. One would think that learning, seemingly involving mostly children, students, and young adults, would not be as important for the national position as economics and disorders. But Dalio shows, convincingly, that learning and education is a close third in determining the positions of nations.

Education helps us, individually, to enjoy prosperity. And it also helps us to engage positively with others. Thus, as individuals, we readily offer sympathy, even help and protection, to others who need it. It reminds me of the story of the Good Samaritan.

Paradoxically, many of us, when joined in education with others in *our own* groups, often see those in need (outsiders in *their* groups) as negatives. Thus, we may go from helping individuals in need, to discriminating against them in groups, wanting to denigrate, attack, jail, kill, even (sometimes) eliminate them.

These ideas lead me to consider what I should have been *doing* in retirement. Not actually *doing* something — I have too little time, too little energy, too little clout, to actually *do* anything. But I could very well, while not being able to *fight* for change, have been able to *wave the flag* for change. At least my ideas are, hopefully, not self-interested, not afraid of the future (which after all, for me, is very short). This means the best I can do is encourage others, you, to take up the cudgels on behalf of learning.

What ideas would I have you most strongly pursue?

The idea that you should push to just **support** learning and education seems so wimpish! **Press, Fight, Attack, Gain, Win**, are much stronger words. Such words are now needed because new, **strong, but dangerous** brands of learning and education have arisen.

What are these new brands?

Mis-Education is one major twisting of learning. Of course, this always did exist, but in relatively minor degree. Today, however, through social media, the internet, artificial intelligence, it is becoming almost the biggest problem. It is pushing so many bad ideas. Especially if it is being used to set different parts of humanity against one another.

Denied Education is another development of learning. Of course, this was also always used in small ways by small groups. It was common enough in history, but it is being especially used today because it can be controlled by rulers. It can keep whole cultures, whole language groups, whole societies, whole tribes, even whole *sexes* and *genders*, in submission!

Rigid Education is yet a third form of learning. Mao Zedong set Government against its own Society by the imposition of rigid Mao thought (summarized in the Little Red Book!). The resulting poverty and famines, disjunctions of families, numbers of deaths in that period were astronomical. Then China seemed to understand the problem and it was relaxed. But now it is undergoing a new recrudescence where people are paid to spy on people, wives and husbands on each other, especially school kids to be tricked into giving family information, workers to spy on their colleagues, and the spying of computer techniques for knowing who everyone is, where they are and what they are saying, even possibly, through AI, what they are thinking! As a result, a new Mao Period, the Xi Jinping Period, of **Rigid Education** has evolved. And this is not just within China itself, but is being forced upon Chinese people outside China throughout the world.

Corrupt Education yet further affects learning. It involves corruption, cheating, stealing and lying through education. Not simply the corruption, cheating, stealing and lying of the young, the dealer, and the criminal, but also of officials and leaders to achieve national and international resurgence over others. The latest forms of this are turning out to include corruption through cybernetics. (In Australia, Robocop may be a particularly bad example.) Whatever good things may flow to humanity from such advances, there are also goodness knows what malevolent possibilities for humanity.

Mind-Bending: telling, instructing, even forcing people what to think is a fifth form of education. This again was probably always evident in small degree in the past, but has become much more evident today. Now it affects many millions in the attempted re-education camps of some nations. Many factors (travel, trade, communications, military powers, internet contacts) increasingly mean that the real power of mind-bending has become complex and worldwide, not simple and local.

Who would have thought that the gentle idea of **learning, of education**, with which we are mostly familiar, could have changed and expanded to include these horrors: **Mis-Education, Denied Education, Rigid Education, Corrupt Education,** and **Mind-Bending Education**? Who would have thought that modifications of simple learning, of education, could have become so damaging?

And these remarks are not aimed in a partisan manner at one or another side of simpler smaller human separations. It is not just a matter of right versus left, elite versus plebs, poor versus rich, powerless versus powerful, governed versus governors, and so on.

Death Wishes

As a result of these forms of education, our present day seems so full of **Death Wishes** (hatreds) between and among so many parts of humanity. Death Wishes exist between nationalities, within governments, among political parties, across populations in societies, religions, communities, even between (and among) sexes, genders, ages, and, especially, in that most dangerous form: in secret. These wishes have led to the creation of barriers: whether religious, psychological, social, or even physical (like iron curtains and bamboo curtains, great walls and Hadrian's walls, Trump walls and Chinese walls). Enmities among humans are so powerful and so widespread.

Life Dreams

Yet humanity really can have **Life Dreams**. We can recognize the complex variations of humans, yes, with peaks that can be easily identified, but, also, yes, with broad valleys that coalesce the peaks into the one overall broad wave that is humanity. This picture is generally supported by people as individuals, but is almost wholly denied by people in groups.

> *As I backward cast my e'e,*
> *the present only toucheth me.*

But forward though I canna see,
I guess and fear.
(modified from Robert Burns).

Future Possibilities

Thus, as I look into the future and guess, I see a former US president, Donald Trump, framing his future campaign as the *next and last battle* against political adversaries. He and his allies are devising plans for a new term to *destroy long-held norms of American democracy*.

He became President the first time largely by attacking *external targets*. They included especially immigrants and immigration, from predominantly Jewish, Muslim, Black, Asian, Mexican, Central and South American, indeed, from almost all other nations (as it suited his purposes).

But now, in his presumed new presidential bid, some of his most vicious and debasing attacks are being levelled at *internal opponents*. He uses language for them that echoes those of authoritarian leaders who rose to power in Germany, Italy and the Soviet Union (in my century). He degrades his internal opponents as "vermin" who need to be "rooted out". "The threat from inside," goes Trump's new voice "is far more sinister, dangerous and grave than the threat from outside". This greater focus on perceived *internal* enemies is a hallmark of current dangerous totalitarian leaders.

Scholars, Democrats, anti-Trump Republicans, many overseas US citizens, and other friends abroad, are now asking new questions. This even applies to American friends in Australia. I was so saddened on meeting, two years ago, a US colleague in our local Australian supermarket, to hear him say: "I am so ashamed *now* to be an American!". How much is Trump comparing himself to the *strongmen* leaders of the past? How much he is copying the overseas *strongmen* of today? Is his rhetoric really in fascist-sounding territory, just his latest public provocation of the left? Or is it a true revelation of his beliefs, revealed by the opening of a curtain, the dropping of a veil?

Trump's allies dismiss these concerns as alarmism from the *swamp*. They say the *vermin* remarks come from reactive liberals whose "sad, miserable existence will be *crushed* when Trump returns to the White House." But, apparently unrealized by them, their own language speaks for itself!

Some experts on authoritarianism have said that Trump's recent words have begun to resemble those used by leaders of the past like Hitler, Mussolini or Stalin. But, in fact, he does not quite mirror those *strongmen of the past*. In fact, he actually seems more to be copying the *strongmen of the present*, like Orbán of Hungary, Erdoğan of Turkey, and, of course, Putin of Russia. But he mostly sees himself as the USA's *strongman of the future*!

But Trump's isolationist views are not really like those that characterized the rule of most overseas autocrats. Although as President, he twisted the power of Congress and the Supreme Court, he was never able to wield the full force of the police, the military, and the secret service, as do other autocrats (though he has tried!). But his approach became angrier and angrier, ending in a deadly riot at the Capitol.

Many people at Trump's events have affirmed his calls to drive out the elected establishment, destroy the real news media, remake government agencies like the Justice Department, and, a new call, *to immolate the challenges of thinking, of learning, of education*. If he wins back the White House, he has said he would have "no choice" but to "imprison" such opponents. He has tested the legal system with broadsides against the integrity of the judiciary, railing against prosecutors, judges, lawyers, and especially interfering in the teaching of teachers, as "politically biased" and "out of control."

The *fake news media* that Trump avers to his people he will destroy, will be replaced by his own truly fake news media! *His people do not flinch at this.*

To the crowds standing amid nearly two dozen American flags at an Independence Day celebration in South Carolina, Trump said: *"The gloves are off"*, while promising retribution against Biden and his family. *His crowd unleashed a resounding cheer.*

"*A sick nest of people* that needs to be cleaned out, and cleaned out immediately" Trump said, about Democrats in Washington. *His supporters roared in approval.*

"Immigration is a very bad thing for us. It's *poisoning the blood* of our country", he says. Apparently unaware that they themselves all derive from migration, they *strongly concur.*

Most countries today are countries of migrants; indeed, in the long term, all countries are countries of migrants!

How much of this rhetoric of Trump is a national majority viewpoint?

In fact, worries about Trump are not only the worries of Democrats. The worries also extend to many Republicans, though they seem to be, in public at least, a minority in the party. "He's absolutely ratcheting it up, and it's very concerning," said John Kasich (Ohio), who ran against him for the Republican presidential nomination in 2016. Kasich further said: "There's just no limit to the anger and hatred in his rhetoric, and this kind of poisonous atmosphere has lowered our standards and hurt our country so much."

Do Trump's rise to power, his ascendancy, and that of many other world leaders with similar political views, signal a worldwide revival of hyper-nationalism and hyper-separatism?

www.ingramcontent.com/pod-product-compliance
Lightning Source LLC
Chambersburg PA
CBHW070308230426
43664CB00015B/2683